BELOVED DEMONS

CONFESSIONS OF AN UNQUIET MIND

C. ANTHONY MARTIGNETTI

INTRODUCTION BY NEIL GAIMAN

3 SWALLYS PRESS
BOSTON, MASSACHUSETTS, USA

Paperback ISBN 978-0-9882300-1-9
1-Memoir 2-Short Stories

To Patricia R. Sanford

("D. Grannie")

Forget safety.
Live where you fear to live.
Destroy your reputation.
Be notorious.
—Rumi

Contents

Acknowledgments

There is no person more worthy of acknowledgment than Nivi Nagiel. Friend, editor and a central creative force of 3 Swallys Press. We laugh and cry our way through these stories, but mostly, we laugh. Truth known, I'm the only one crying, in part because she focused on the Stoics for her master's in philosophy and is able to find the sense and the good in most moments. But, how she puts up with me is a miracle beyond any philosophy. Niv, thanks.

My friend Neil Gaiman for his help and encouragement, always wise counsel, brilliant and unique gifts from across the sea, and for writing the introduction to this book. Also, for taking such good care of my wonderful friend who is next . . .

Amanda Palmer, without whom my life could well be devoid of art and creative endeavor. Often without saying it, she challenges me and many others in her wide circle to stand up, deliver and make art. She's one who has stuck by me through the most dense and frightening of times and enjoyed enormous fun with me over decades. I love her for that and countless other reasons. Always.

The Souled Out Artists (SOA) for their willingness to bear stories in unbearable states of development, for reading and giving feedback beyond the call, and for encouraging me to write when I feel I cannot.

A special acknowledgment to Paul Trainor in the SOA group for being my steady friend, for being the IT man for 3 Swallys Press and for incarnating the books. Fleshless as they may be on the screen, he actually brings them to physical life. His friendship, mad humor and encouragement bring me to life too.

Beloved Demons (and *Lunatic Heroes*) got blurbed by the best people. People I admire and learn from through their counsel and their writings. Each of them was very busy and still generous with their words and time despite demanding, often international, schedules. I am honored. Thank you all.

I would be remiss to not mention you, my reader. Thank you on behalf of *Lunatic Heroes* and now, for reading this newest madness. Thank you for trusting me with your time and heart. Without you I'd just be in a café scribbling in a journal and getting nowhere because of constant interference by thoughts of my own relentless insignificance and never-to-be-discovered greatness. Thank you again.

My wife Laura, who bears my dark moods, my infantile narcissism, my reluctance to engage in anything social, my easy dissatisfaction, my regular inappropriateness, my roiling and seething (often thinly disguised) anger and for still thinking I'm the funniest guy in her bed.

Thou hast saved me.

C. Anthony Martignetti
October 21, 2013

Eight Views of Mount Fuji:

An Introduction to *Beloved Demons*

I.

It's all about life.

And in the midst of whatever else we're in, it's always about life.

II.

I had known Amanda Palmer for six months, and we were going on our first date. Our first date was four days long, because it was all the free time we had at the beginning of 2009 and we were giving it to each other. I had not yet met her family. I barely knew her friends.

"I want you to meet Anthony," she said.

It was January. If I'd really known who Anthony was in her life then, if I'd known how much he'd played his part in raising her, I think I would have been nervous. I wasn't nervous. I was just pleased that she wanted to introduce me to someone that she knew.

Anthony, she told me, was her next door neighbour. He had known her since she was a child.

He turned up in the restaurant: a tall, good-looking man who looked a decade younger than his age. He had a walking cane, an easy comfortable manner, and we talked all that evening. Anthony told me about the nine-year-old Amanda who had thrown snowballs at his window, and about the teenage Amanda who had come next door when she needed to vent, and about the college-age Amanda who had called him from Germany when she was lonely and knew nobody, and about rockstar Amanda (it was Anthony who had named the Dresden Dolls). He asked me about me, and I answered him as honestly as I could.

Later, Amanda told me that Anthony liked me, and had told her he thought I would make a good boyfriend for her.

I had no idea how important this was, or what Anthony's approval meant at the time.

III.

Life is a stream: an ongoing conversation of nature with itself, contradictory and opinionated and dangerous. And the stream is made up of births and deaths, of things that come into existence and pass away. But there is always life, and things feeding on life.

We had been married for five months. Amanda phoned me in tears from a yoga retreat in the Canary Islands, to tell me Anthony had leukemia. She flew home. Anthony began treatment. It didn't look as if there was anything real to worry about. Not then. They can treat these things.

As the next year began, Amanda recorded an album, *Theatre is Evil*. She started touring for it, a planned tour that would take the best part of a year.

At the end of the summer, Anthony's leukemia took a turn for the worse, and suddenly there were very real reasons to worry. He would need to go for chemo. He might not make it. We read the Wikipedia entry on the kind of leukemia Anthony had, and we learned that this was not the kind you get better from, and we were sobered and scared.

Amanda had been a touring rock musician for a decade, and took pride in not cancelling gigs. She called me, and she cancelled the second half of her tour to be with Anthony. We took a house in Cambridge's Harvard

Square so she could be close to him.

We had a small dinner for friends, shortly after we moved in, to celebrate the birthday of Anthony's wife, Laura. Laura is very beautiful, and very gentle, and a lawyer who helps people who cannot help themselves. I cooked fish for them. Pat, Laura's mother, came, and helped me cook.

That was a year ago.

IV.

Anthony had been Amanda's friend. Somewhere in there, while she and I were dating, before we were married or even engaged, he became someone I talked to when I was lost and confused and way out of my depth in the thickets of a relationship that was always like nothing I'd ever known before. I called him from Australia and texted him from a train in New Mexico. His advice was wise and practical, and often—mostly—it was right.

He stopped me overthinking things; would offer hope, always with a matter-of-fact thread of darkness and practicality: yes, you can fix *this*, but you'll have to learn to live with *that*.

I discovered over the years to come that many of the things I treasured most about Amanda were gifts that Anthony had given her or taught her over the years of their friendship.

One night Amanda read me a story that Anthony had written, about his childhood, about food, about love. It was gripping. I asked for more.

With a mixture of nervousness and diffidence, Anthony gave me more of his stories to read: autobiographical sketches and confessionals, some funny, some dark. Each of the stories shone a light inside Anthony's skull and showed the reader the view from his past. He was nervous because I write books for a living, and he was relieved (I think) that I liked them.

I liked them very much.

I had worried that we would have nothing in common, apart from our love of Amanda. I was wrong. We both had a fascination with, and a delight in stories. Do not give either of us gifts: give us the tale that accompanies the gift. That is what makes the gift worth having.

Ask Anthony about the walking canes I gave him. The joys of the gifts are in the stories.

V.

I'm thinking about all those signs we put on our walls when we were teenagers and knew that we would live forever, in order to show how tough and cynical and worldly-wise we were:

NOBODY GETS OUT OF HERE ALIVE was one of them. THE PERSON WHO DIES WITH THE MOST TOYS WINS was another. There was one of two vultures sitting on a branch that said PATIENCE MY ASS, I'M GONNA KILL SOMETHING.

And it's easy to be cynical about death when you're young. When you are young, death is an anomaly. It's not real. It only affects other people. It's a bullet you'll dodge easily: it's why young people can go into battle. They really *will* live forever. They know.

As you stick around, as you go around the earth, you realise that life is an ever-narrowing conveyor belt. Slowly, inexorably, it takes us all along with it, and one by one we tumble off the sides of the conveyor belt into darkness.

A few days after Amanda decided that she was going to stop touring and be with Anthony, we heard that our friend Becca Rosenthal had died. She was 27. She was young and beautiful and filled with life and potential. She wanted to be a librarian.

Just before Christmas, our friend Jeremy Geidt went into hospital for a relatively minor operation. Jeremy was a crusty, foul-mouthed, gloriously funny actor and teacher who had come to the US in the early 60s with Peter Cook's Establishment Club. He had lived a remarkable life, which he would tell us about in booze-tinged anecdotes and perfectly deployed expletives. Jeremy spent most of the next six months in the hospital, recovering from the first operation, and dealing with a tumour in his throat. He died in August, suddenly and unexpectedly. He was old, but he relished life, chewed it like a dog with a rawhide bone.

They fall off the conveyor belt into the darkness, our friends, and we cannot talk to them any more.

In November, Anthony's friends divided up the tasks of taking him to chemo, staying with him, bringing him home again (he could not drive himself back, after all). I offered to help, but Amanda said no.

VI.

I met Amanda Palmer because she wanted help in playing dead. She had been pretending to be dead in photographs for the previous 14 years, and now she was making a whole record about it. *Who Killed Amanda Palmer*, it was called. We met and interacted because she wanted someone to write stories of her deaths.

I found the idea intriguing.

I wrote stories. I killed her over and over again in every story and poem. I even killed her on the back of the record. I wrote a dozen different Amanda Palmers before I ever knew her, each of them dying in a dozen or more inventive ways.

The deaths were inevitable. Of course, sometimes describing and thinking about death is our way of celebrating life. Of feeling more alive. Of grasping life tightly, licking it, tasting it, plunging our teeth into it and knowing that we are part of it. It's like sex, the tumbling into the tugging and pulling of the continuous stream of life. And life and sex are always tied in to death: the erection on the gallows, the final urge to procreate and live before the darkness.

We behave differently when we see the darkness looming. We become creatures of lust and fear.

Amanda pushed and helped him, and Anthony published some of his stories in a collection called *Lunatic Heroes*. He and his friends Nivi and Paul formed 3 Swallys Press to bring the book to the world. The launch event for *Lunatic Heroes*, in Lexington, MA, Anthony's hometown, was a dark event in a sold-out theatre: Amanda read her introduction, and I read some of *The Ocean at the End of the Lane*, and most of all Anthony read from *Lunatic Heroes*.

I worried that he wasn't going to live much beyond the launch event.

I was scared for Laura, Anthony's wife, and scared for Amanda. I knew that any sadness I was going to feel at the loss of my friend was going to have to be put aside while I looked after Amanda, who would be broken and torn by Anthony's death.

It was going to be hard for all of us.

I felt the air from the wings of the angel of death brushing my face at that launch event, that night.

VII.

Life has a sense of humour, but then again, so does death.

Laura's mother, Pat, who helped me cook when we first moved into this house, died this year of leukemia.

Anthony, to our delight, got through the chemo, and, with the help of a newly released drug, he recovered. He is in remission—for now. He beat death, as much as any of us gets to beat death. For now—it's always a transient win, that one, and the reaper can wait. She's patient, and she will be here when the last of us has gone.

Anthony no longer had leukemia; but now he had a book called *Lunatic Heroes*.

There were darker stories that Anthony had crafted from his life that had not made it into that first book. Stories of obsession and desire. Stories of loss and fear and hate. The kind of stories that need you to be brave to tell them, braver still to publish them so that other people can look inside your head and know what makes you tick, and what makes you hard, and what makes you cry, that tell you that the hardest battles are the ones you fight inside your own head, when nobody else is going to know if you won or lost or even if a battle was fought at all.

Or to put it another way, and quote the Buddha, who knew about these things,

> Though one may conquer a million men in battle, yet the noblest of victors is he who conquers himself. Self-conquest is far better than the conquest of others. Not even a god, an angel, Mara or Brahma could turn that triumph back into defeat.

VIII.

We win some, but we lose many. We lose a lot. We lose our friends and we lose our family. In the end we lose everything. No matter who's with us, we always die alone. When you fight your battles, whatever battles you fight, it's always going to be about life.

We leave behind two things that matter, Stephen Sondheim said, in a musical I love and Amanda doesn't, and those two things are children and art.

Anthony's children are scattered: they are the people whose lives he has influenced and helped to shape. I count my wife as one of his children. Anthony's art is here, in these pages, waiting for you, as fresh, as sharp, as painful a hundred years from now when I'm dead and Anthony's dead and Amanda's dead and everyone we know is dust and ash and bones in the ground.

This book is a gift: and, as I said, it is the tales that accompany the gift that matter: the stories that show us the joy of event, of the shaping of memories, and the joy of a life lived, as all lives are lived, both in the light and in the darkness.

These pages are gifts, from Anthony to you, and they hold the tales that accompany the gifts, from someone who has walked into the darkness and now stands in the light, ready to tell you his stories.

Neil Gaiman
November 12, 2013

Cocoon Talk: *Confessions of a Psychology Intern*

"Musta hit him," I muttered, seeing a butterfly glide in front of the truck grill one hot afternoon. It was summertime 20 years ago, and I was rolling down the on-ramp to Route 2 in Belmont, listening to Tom Waits on the radio and heading toward the final interview for a predoctoral fellowship at Boston University. Looking back in the side view mirror, I thought I actually saw its final flutter on the asphalt.

"Sorry," I said out the window. This, I interpreted as a sign of summer's end. A familiar tension churned in my stomach, accompanied by an image of the wind whipping through my clothes while I fumble with numb, spastic fingers to get the top button done up. A picture of trees standing grim, silent, and as barren as the year the gypsy moths ate every leaf in Massachusetts. My eyes were a little watery; I often got choked up listening to Waits anyway, so I was already vulnerable to remorse for involuntary bug slaughter.

"If it was December, it would be almost dark by now." I often spoke as if someone was in the car with me. It was just like me to go morose when any death reminders came up. I'd start talking about the dark and darkness, cold and loneliness, aging and illness, money, and how the hell can anybody keep making a living through a whole lifetime? I'd get myself all wound up and just rattle on in my head about the scariest shit I could think of. I tried to bounce back and accept responsibility for the little body, waving lifelessly, on the street. It's been said that the end of the world for a caterpillar is a butterfly to us. What, I wondered, was the end of the world for a butterfly? I was afraid I was seeing it.

"Okay, it wasn't my fault, and it's only August 6th—still summer—the internship doesn't even begin until September 9th." I began to wonder if butterflies had hearts. "I think I'm mental!" I shouted at the steering wheel.

It would have been a stretch to believe I was a PhD candidate, planning to become a clinical fellow at the fanciest mental health center in the city.

There were legitimate questions.

Question Number One: Would I ever grow up?

There was no evidence based on my behavior. I'm a lot older than I act. Who else, in the wide world, would be crying over Tom Waits and talking to butterflies? I was always babbling, always unsure of what I was saying yet revealing nothing, and never really trusted people who said they knew themselves or suggested that they knew me. Never really wanted anyone to see me.

My father, Joe, thought he knew me. "I'm lookin' right tru you," he'd proclaim. He once said, at the beach during a family vacation, "On paper you might look all right but you got nothin' really goin' for yourself. What are you gonna do wit your life Mistah?" He called me "Mistah" when he was winding up to fire serious shock waves against my earthly existence. He thought he was Mr. Huge. As soon as he began his squawk list, I ran backwards into the ocean and fell in, holding my heart, like I was zapped by a ray gun. He always killed me. He then turned to my sister, I later found out, and said, "Does he seem almost 30 to you? I can't believe it—he acts like he's 16." That was some years ago. Mr. Huge has tied his boat to another shore since. But, I *was* quite immature. Some people think we messed up with one another. Everybody's got an opinion. I let others be the judge. Me, I couldn't care less. I'm good like that.

I never could quite shake Joe, though.

I don't forget the moment when Billy, my oldest friend, grabbed my hand and pulled me to the end of the driveway where my brother Michael was standing and crying. Billy had been visiting. He'd just heard the news in the house, before it got to me. Though we had been buddies since high school, he didn't want to be the one to say the words.

"He's dead," my brother said. I heaved inward and reached blind for his hand with Billy's help.

"He's dead," he said again, and then moaned out what I was holding in. We stood, leaned on each other, at the bottom of the driveway with Billy watching, and we rocked together . . . with the rest of our world.

My father was 61. He died from a stroke that began on Father's Day, just before Michael and I met him where he played golf. We were going to lunch and then clothes shopping for him. He had separated from my mother, Jackie, seven months earlier, after 40 years of marriage, and needed some looking after during that time. We knew he'd pay for the clothes, and buy us some in the bargain. But that day he wasn't himself. He was slurring his speech and losing his balance and forgetting things he had just said a moment earlier. We took him to the hospital, and he died there, after lapsing into a coma two weeks later.

I still hate saying he's dead, and can't get used to the word. Instead I say, "He left for good," or "He's reincarnating," or whatever pops into my head. The difficulty is definitely about his being gone, but it's also death in general. Sometimes I feel the rank sound of death in my ear like a whisper from Joe. I don't think I ever got a handle on exactly how much death, and his in particular, freaked me out. I gotta forget about it. Gotta put it out of my mind.

Two weeks after Joe's funeral, I was watching a great prizefight on television and picked up the phone to tell him to watch. A couple of numbers into dialing, I realized he was gone. That was the moment I exhaled the breath I drew at the end of the driveway. I needed to talk with Joe, wanted to hear his voice one more time and dialed again to get his machine, but there was only a recording from the phone company. Flattened by the reality of never hearing him again, I lay back on the couch and assumed the position referred to in hatha yoga as the "corpse pose" and began thinking that when people you care about die, it can be a good idea to keep their answering machines on for a while. This way you could leave them a message like, "Dad, I still need you."

BOSTON 12 MILES. "Jesus." Signs like that were always such a surprise to me. I hardly paid attention when I drove. The freaking clinic interview was 25 minutes away, and I was in wonderland, where I used to live a lot of the time back then.

Wake up, Mistah! Where's your head? Joe would show up in the passenger seat with a querulous and critical expression frozen on his face. He was usually inquiring about the location of my head as well as the direction it was going.

"Hit the AC." Heat made me anxious. It's still a thing with me, the heat.

Mistah Snow Job, my father called me. *Throwin' curve balls all the time.* He didn't know me, not like he used to. I took that as a kind of compliment. But at least he saw me enough to know I was hiding from him. The Invisible Man, that was me. I dreamed of being invisible as a kid. This way I could get to know everybody else, and what they really thought of me, and could hear their private sentences while watching them undress. Yeah, well. Don't judge me. What would you do?

So there I sat, a butterfly killer, mourning to the accompaniment of a heart-broken balladeer. And all the while tentatively becoming a psychologist.

"SEDUCER!" I was screaming in the damn car like those twitching, drug-crazed, shirtless characters in the back of police cars on *COPS.* I've always thought I had a mild case of Tourette's syndrome. Twitch and shout. Blurt things out like I'm battling a tic disorder. I needed to get that seducer idea out of my head; it wouldn't mix well with all the shrinks—too close to being an abuser. It's like I'm Nabokov in my mind. In the age of victim mania, you have to be careful what you say; people might think they know you. Before you realize it, all the

women would start recovering memories and accusing
me of satanic rituals. Then I'd be diagnosed with some
mix of multiple personality, ADD, chronic fatigue and
carpel tunnel for chrissake. It was getting ridiculous with
the phonetic disorders, road rage, fibromyalgia and
PTSD. What did all that mean? And why was I going
into a field that ascribed to so much malarkey? Well, for
protection, I was determined not to let people really see
me. I'd be the Invisible Man for once and for all, and
stay young so at least my heart wouldn't turn on me.

It's popular, the desire to stay young. But for me it
had a peculiar twist. I often felt there was someone with
me or in me. Not really someone else, but a younger
version of me. Thinner, more wiry, able to take stairs
two, three at a time. That other one who ran beside me,
bounding along, while I slammed the pavement like a bag
of ham. He was happier, more free. I knew that young
one, or "Kid" I sometimes called him. I liked him. I
relied on him. I needed him for force and anger and
speed. I got the idea of Kid from reading one of my
favorite poets, Antonio Machado. Machado had the
notion of "another one" in his poems. He wrote, "I talk
always to the man who walks along with me." Then, in
another:

Look for your other half
who walks always next to you
and tends to be what you aren't.

It was partly from these ideas that Kid popped out. He was not always apart from me; we were one for the longest time, but he was born separate out of need. It was a painful birth.

He started to show occasionally when I lived in Canada after high school, and by the time I was 25, he was with me full-time. I got the feeling there was a crowd in there with Kid though. I think all the fighting I witnessed in the family room while growing up set the stage for him and the rest of them to come on board and frolic in the bloody aftermath. I carried a mess of characters with me then. Crazy man. Crazy.

Driving along, I wondered about the internship at the clinic. I was constantly anxious about imagined confrontations with feminists. My language was often sexist and politically offensive. I couldn't stop myself from saying whatever came into my mind. I'm like a monkey. It's the tic disorder. I was sure there would be lesbians and transsexuals, people from other cultures, academics and existentialists, and people whose eyes remain pervadingly fixed on yours and who hardly respond when you talk to them. I was planning my defense. I'd be sure they knew I was there. Visible yet invisible. Hiding in plain sight. I'd have to mark my territory. Lead with the jab—*Pop-Pop-Bing-Bang-BOOM* with the left hook to finish—there you go. Look at you now. *Muthafukka.* Look. At. You. Now.

Well at least I wasn't recovering from anything. I didn't need Twelve Steps. I took steps: psychotherapy twice a week for five years, per the graduate program's recommendation, and eight months of Reichian therapy thrown in. I read the books, wrote the papers and was about to begin a two-year clinical fellowship. I paid my dues. So what, I was insecure. Sue me. I mean it's not like I bludgeon baby seals.

Here, I was into a full-blown argument with myself while barreling down the road to the city. I spent half my life back then justifying myself in my head, and the other half regretting the time wasted doing it. At least I'd begun to occasionally notice it; that should've counted for something. I started to pep talk myself down Route 2.

"I'm okay—I can do this. What's the big deal—lots of people go through the training and become shrinks. Why should I be any different? I'm no clown." By now I had all but forgotten the butterfly and Waits.

I was feeling mildly self-assured when I noticed something dimly familiar happening. I was only then becoming able to sense it. It was as if my body had disappeared. No torso, no Jeep, no highway, just the hurtling-head. Torso, truck and road all transformed into a numb rubber corpse, there to transport the head and its sentences. The Jeep was a vehicle for the body, the body a vehicle for the skull-chatter. I ended up staring blankly through the windshield like those old men in

West Palm Beach. My breathing was so shallow I was practically suffocating myself. I somehow lived for years with barely enough oxygen, with the life squeezed out of my chest as if by a vise. I'd feel right at home on top of Everest with those other clowns who climb into thin air and die.

Air seems fine. Nice and cool, too. Ahh, I love the mountains.

Chip, my shrink, was the first to actually mention it.

"I notice that you seem to go away at certain times in our discussions," he said one morning. He was like some fumbling archaeologist who bumped into the Fortress of Solitude, that fantastic castle Superman kept under the ice at the North Pole. Chip rang the doorbell of my safe house. *Hold it now! What's this? Session's almost up,* I thought.

"What? Me? What? . . . No! I was just thinking," I blurted in response.

"Oh?" Chip replied with that $100-per-45-minute precision that reflected years of training.

"What? No, nuthin', I don't know, I was just thinkin'."

"It seemed as if you sort of disappeared there for a moment," he pretended to reframe his observation. He was a pit bull with no teeth. A nervous, pathetic little miniature pit bull.

"Who? Me? No, I'm here."

"Oh, okay." He let my arm slip out through his tiny,

jittery, inflamed gums.

"Well maybe next time we can talk about what happens when you seem to go away like that." His parting comment was tantamount to a curse.

"Okay," I said and immediately started whistling some barely audible cacophony while gathering my stuff as though I was mincing through a moonlit cemetery.

When I left his office a few minutes later, I started reciting T.S. Eliot. I did that when I couldn't find my own sentences. "Do I dare disturb the universe? . . . I am no prophet—and here's no great matter; I have seen the moment of my greatness flicker, and I have seen the eternal Footman hold my coat, and snicker, and in short, I was afraid."

I had been busy with a lifelong project of pulling the wool over my eyes, while thinking it was others who couldn't see me. Tangled in my own yarn. I got shaken a little, but that was all right. I wasn't gonna let the likes of Chip mess me up. Weasel.

"Fuck Chip anyway, he's workin' for *me*."

Chip always seemed to be waiting for me to retrieve some major scene . . . satanic ritual abuse, alien abduction, priestly molestation, dental malpractice, carpal tunnel. *Whatevah.*

"I DON'T REMEMBER!" I always startled myself when I was alone and shouted out shit like that. Gilles de la Tourette. I'd occasionally realize that I was driving the car without the aid of conscious awareness, something I had been doing since my learner's permit.

"Asleep at the wheel," Joe would say to characterize my life in the world. I was weaving around like a hundred-year-old. Getting ready for West Palm. Nearly drove under a trailer truck.

"JESUS! I coulda been there with the butterfly." I always came to that. My own heart's final flutter. Death. The last call. "The bitter end," as his sister Emma said when Joe finally went to the other side. "I was with him to the bitter end, honey."

I've always basically been scared—scared of life and death; scared, especially, that something was horribly wrong with me. Alone with my own dreadful secrets in the Fortress. At the same time, I always felt I was special. Great. Potentially. So I put myself around a bunch of people who spend their lives looking for something wrong with everybody. Might as well just hang around with Joe.

Question Number Two: Would I ever really make the grade? This was the real thing here. Dr. me. Holy flying shitballs!

No more farting around just working in drug rehab clinics. Those places where most of the staff bullshit along with a line of unproved addiction theory and tell the patients to take the cotton out of their ears and stick it in their mouths, pay up and then go to AA.

Not at the fancy-ass clinic I was heading toward, no. There would be 20 supervising shrinks there. They, being dedicated to helping the terrified of the world deconstruct their personal protections. Those jokers spend their lives looking for the keys to everyone's Fortress except their own, because they have the best security system of all: "I'm a psychologist, and therefore have all my shit together." Nobody, and I mean nobody, is fooled, people.

Thank God for protections, I suppose. Without them, we would never have the strength to get stuck at those key stages of development so that we can establish a transference reaction with a therapist later in life. *Yee-haw!*

"Fuck Chip anyway!" What mumbo jumbo. You'd have to be Frank Lloyd Wright to figure out the architecture of the thing. Victim mania, as far as I was concerned. So, of all possibilities, this was my professional quest. How in the world, I wondered, did this goal become mine? I wasn't like those other nerds. I'd never truly fit in, and that seemed good.

"What the hell am I doing in this business?" I said, speaking up to the rearview. I spent as much time looking at that mirror as I did through the windshield. That was perfect me, really. I'd been doing counseling work for almost 10 years at that point and—except for internship, comps and dissertation—almost a PhD, and I felt better suited to sell a rodent's rectum to a blind man for a pinkie ring than to pull myself out of an anxious moment.

Arlington, Cambridge, Alewife Station all went by in dream sequences. There was a vague awareness of greenery, houses, a huge gray wall, going past off-ramps, under overpasses. The city was there, floating in the distance, like a dreary Shangri-La. At the same time, I saw none of it. I may have remembered it from having passed through on so many instances before. I just thought. That's what I did. I lived exclusively from the neck up.

I might as well have jogged to the city, for all the effort it took thinking all the time. I always lived in my head, but beginning to notice it drained the life out of me. I was like a dead man who didn't have the sense to stiffen up. I wasn't ready to awaken, and certainly not ready to remember anything nasty or weird. Someone once said, *"We wake exhausted."* My face dropped just thinking about waking up. Hardly any breathing going on at all back then.

"Breathe, breathe, breathe," I reminded myself, with Kid's help, and, once again, felt my hands on the wheel. Kid did CPR from time to time, just to keep the show on the road. Hands lightly but firmly gripped, foot on the pedal, ass in the seat. Okay, Harvard Stadium. I was driving again; body-mind-self was driving. Total driving.

Feeling really real. Holistic awareness. Evenly hovering awareness.

Immediately I thought, where's Waits? Oooh my balls! Radio—crotch. One moment of present awareness and I was desperate for a distraction.

Get a grip, Mistah!

"Shut up Joe, Christ." I was certain I had at least a mild case of Tourette's. I did get these urges in my crotch area though, especially in the summer. It was so bad, I had no control—I'd attack my groin like a badger.

I used to try to meditate in this religious organization I joined for a while, and as soon as I sat down on the cushion with all the others around me, the urge to shift to the crotch would start. It was always hot in the room. Made me anxious. Could hardly breathe. I tried to think of the crotch-call as a chance to practice discipline and self-control. After 10 seconds I'd be flying away at my belt trying to get my hands in there. I was always in a fit.

Maybe Joe was right about me having done nothing with my life. And it was already too late to die young. Shit! I never changed much over those years, and in that way I was a lot like poor Joe. Nothing much changed for him but the channels on TV. I missed him. He missed me. Most of my relationship with him was in my head. Maybe it was the same for him.

Joe lived in me. I carried him wherever I went. All sexual thoughts were somehow tied up with him, anything related to money or work, or whenever I had to deal with or confront men, Joe appeared—thankfully, along with Kid. I needed Kid for toughness and courage. Kid would rattle the bushes and shake the trees like a baby gorilla hoping to frighten off potential threats. I was relying on him for help with those things, but truth told, he really didn't have a lot going for himself either.

Like one of the times I drove in Maine, on a 12-mile stretch of road tucked into the woods called the Airline Route. I have no idea why it was called that.

The Maniacs would say, "Most dangerous strip of road in New England, *ayuh*." It was an unlit, narrow, winding, pockmarked serpent going two ways. Unguarded death-falls on either side, strewn with animal carcasses—foxes, coons, even dogs. I drove it many times, but the only time I ever drove it in daylight, I noticed tiny white crosses along the roadside marking fatal crash sites. Every other time it was pitch dark—cats couldn't see, and bats couldn't hear the faint radio stations I happened upon. Waits says you gotta die with the radio on. *Ayuh*.

"One hour trip at the fastest, wintahtime," the Maniacs would say. "Choose your ruts wisely, you'll be in 'em for the next 12 miles."

I hitchhiked and drove through Maine to Canada, where I lived on my own for a few years. Halifax, Nova Scotia. Found my way there in an old Karmann Ghia convertible a number of times. I did a lot of living in my head in those parts of the world too. Skull-chatter. My mobile home.

A tiny general store stayed open late a few miles before the Airline. I stopped there six or so times over a three-year period for food and entertainment. The men in the store—huge, toothless, bearded types with checkered shirts and filthy baseball caps—were terrifying. They'd look at me. My hair was long. I was thin and couldn't grow a beard for shit. Just some straggled hairs floating, inscrutably, under my chin—looked like a brown-haired Chinaman.

I prayed there would be no women in the store; no spandexed bottle-blonds in platform shoes, with too much makeup, lipstick from ear to ear. Once, while I was in the place, this horrendous broad said to a group of bruisers hulking near the store entrance, "I think he's lookin' at me." The men turned and stiffened in my direction like a cluster of dicks. I was in Fiji land with a bunch of cannibals as far as I was concerned, and even if I got to the car, they could cut the ragtop open and pull me out by the head. Then they would scare me to death with some hideous dance they'd do, eat me, pick my bones clean and use them as crosses on the Airline

Route. That was the level of imagining going on back then. See, you think I'm kidding?

Poised for a crisis on each visit to the store, I would silently go about my business of buying junk food and pornography. That, I was sure, ingratiated me with the regulars. I always bought three or four normal magazines so as not to appear a total pervert. They had some really nasty ones. This place was way north; it had to satisfy the likes of alcoholic lumberjacks, displaced Inuit and the inbred. *Leather Thrashin' Motorcycle Mamas* was, if memory serves, one of the classics that I sandwiched between *Popular Mechanics* and *Farmers' Almanac.* The proprietor, a gentleman in his late hundreds, would look over at the others while ringing up the smut. He was in a wheelchair, so I was tempted not to look at him.

When I was a kid, my mother would whisper, while squeezing my hand with a chiropractic grip, "Hunny, don't look at that crippled boy, hunny, it's not nice." I couldn't help it. As I passed the child, I'd walk, rigid as a zombie; the skin of my face stretched back, my eyes torqued to the corner of my face, head straight forward. I wanted to look at him so bad. I threw my eyes like an ocular ventriloquist. It was the same looking at the guy in the store. Trying to appear not to be, but actually gawking and looking like a mental patient while doing it.

At the Airline store, I'd become dizzy with anxiety whenever one of the men even cleared his throat. God forbid if one of the women looked as if she might gesture in my direction. A coy wave, a raised brow, a wink or a smile is all it would take to catapult me into a panic. One of the ladies once said, "Bye hunny," as I was readying to leave. My knees turned to gel packs, I started losing my balance and walked slowly, without direction, like a tranquilized orangutan. It was a bad dream. I thought I was going to fall down right on the old plank floor, too weak to get up, squirting pee with every attempt. All of them circling around me, doing their perverted square dance. I'd have to watch, paralyzed, while they hit me with tuna bats. Thank God Kid made enough of an appearance to at least get me out of the store and into the car. Jesus H., what guilt for a lousy porno mag. "DON'T EAT ME!"

It's heinous; there I was screaming "Don't eat me" on my way to being a psychology intern. I was fucked. My mind was not my own. I was neurotic at the very best. Christ, I really used to frighten myself with the variety and depth of my pathologies. Instead of the internship clinic, I should have driven straight to the emergency room at Mount Auburn and seen if they had a place available for me in the bin.

"Hi, I'm Oedipus. Do you have a room?" I shouldn't have even been allowed to drive there. Maybe I'd have to hitchhike to the hospital with a hand-drawn Crayola sign: **"Psychotic . . . need ride . . . will not harm self."**

After escaping with my life from the Maniac store, and in the safety of the car, I would head out into the black Maine woods, toward the Canadian border. Out of sight of the men and their ladies, I would drink, eat, drive and look at the porno under the interior light. A manic juggling act. Once I negotiated a good chunk of the Airline that way. Probably more than once. No seat belt. After stuffing my face with Table Talk mini blueberry pies, I'd locate the pictures I liked best and play with myself while driving. Once or twice I had Homeric orgasms. Maybe more than a couple of times. I shot all over the place like a monkey peeing. No concern for anything. I spoke in tongues, let go of the wheel and screeched like an idiot. Weaving and cumming on the Airline.

"Worst place to weave and cum in New England." Ayuh. Chip thought I had a death wish. He was a friggin' weirdo. *Die?* I'm trying to have a squirt here. Gimme a break, die.

I used to fear that one of the local constabulary might pull me over just after or even, God forbid, during the depraved merriment. It probably would have been an auxiliary or volunteer cop, maybe one of the guys from the store who had been following me, "out lookin' for a snack" with his lady riding shotgun, putting lipstick over her cheekbones. "Hunny, hi hunny." It might as well have been my parents following me. Born guilty.

At this point, there was no thought to the road whatsoever during that trip to the clinic; I was driving there in a reverse fugue state. Remembering nothing *but* my past. No idea where I might have presently been, really. For a moment, I had a vague realization that the Jeep was speeding to Boston, under its own supervision, my face as blank as a dog behind the wheel. I checked the rearview to see the dog-face every now and then, and weaved dizzy all over the road while looking in the mirror. Danger to myself and others. I'd fail a mental status evaluation:

"Hello, I'm going to ask you a few questions, sir. Okay?"

"Okay."

"Have you seen Elvis?"

"You mean Elvis Presley?"

"Yes, Presley. Do you speak with Elvis?"

"Ahhhh . . . "

"Is Kid here? The young one who is always with you?"

"AHHHH! Kid? I . . . I . . . how do you . . . ?"

"Can you let the young one speak now?"

The young one *was* probably with me. We were safe, I guess. I think Kid is immortal. I hope so. Jesus jumpin' Christ, I hope so. I often thought that if I lost Kid, I'd just exist, raw and under threat with each human encounter.

I usually drove in a dissociated state—psychobabble for not being there—Chip's word. Chip and Joe were all over the freakin' Jeep. Joe was forever nodding at Chip for consensus, with a face that said, *See, he's gone! Completely GONE!* I've lived most of my life not being there. I'd have conversations, watch TV, have sex, drive . . . lots of things—zoned out—went through high school and college that way, attended every mass like that. Maybe that's what Chip meant when he said I seem to go away. Even Kid was distracted from time to time. He ran around—great energy but it was all over the place. All juice, no technique.

But I was nothing compared to Joe. Mr. Huge. Talk about distracted; he was so out of it he'd pee in his pants five times a year at least. He also would rush into the house seconds before taking a dump in his work clothes and make the hall toilet just in time. He could have used those huge adult diapers for the incontinent when he was about 40. *"Hey kids, anybody seen my Pull-Ups? Hurry up, I gotta get to work. You think money grows on trees? Hah?"*

I couldn't feel much of anything except angry and scared back in those middle years with Joe. You wouldn't know it, though. I was a pissed-off little chickenshit in a brave suit. *"C'mon, I'm here. What are you lookin' at? I'm right here. You wanna fuck wit me?"* Tough guy. Big words. All the while I was developing a prolapsed rectum. Knees rattling like castanets.

Another time, I was driving to Canada on a miserable night, after a major blowout with Joe hours before. Fiddling with the radio dials, I couldn't find anything but a couple of fuzzy stations, mostly in French, when suddenly one came in perfectly clear. The opening line of the song playing was "Golden days in the sunshine of my flaming youth." It was the first time I had ever heard those words coming from anywhere but Joe's mouth. He had been singing it to me since I was a kid. It may have been the only line he knew. He would sing: "Goldendays in da sunshine of my flamin' yout," with what he thought was a happy face that made him look sad to me. It was as if he had just finished a great aria that had moved him to cry. It brought Joe right into the car that night. Sitting next to me, looking straight ahead, with one thick tear painting a slow path of disappointment down his face. Right there between the Coke bottles and pie boxes. Right there with the Leather Thrashin' Mamas and my joint, swollen in my jeans.

"Pop! Where are you? What happened for chrissake? I'm sorry. I never meant to be this way." He always killed me.

I finally realized that I was entering Boston. Big buildings were a dead giveaway. My crotch started acting up, and at that point I was yelling like a stock trader in the pit. I felt as twisted driving to the clinic just thinking about that song as I did back then when it happened.

Well, I never cried so hard in my life when that came on the radio, except on that hot night, years ago, when Joe left for good, and the tears tasted just the same.

The bitter end.

I arrived in a sweat at Bay State Road, number 185, The Danielsen Institute. Time to re-associate, re-constitute, re-compensate, all the psychobabble I could muster. I was amazed I didn't puke on the way in. What an ordeal. There was a parking space right in front. Two bicycles leaned together, locked to the tree. Classy street. Okay, things were good; it was a clear, hot August afternoon, 4:28 p.m. I'd always felt confident in myself for at least being on time.

"Never late." I, of course, was muttering to myself as I left the Jeep. I became concerned that someone from the Danielsen Institute building had seen me talking to myself. That was me back then. Both talking to myself and paranoid about it. So, naturally, I had to pretend that I was actually singing to myself, and wanted the words to be consistent with what I just said in case anyone might be studying my every articulation from the windows. Scrutinizing the lip movements of people in the street was, I was sure, what they did all day at that place.

"*Ferreting out pathology in every pedestrian:* that's our motto here at the Institute."

I started singing anyway. *"Never late, neverlate baby, nevernever late, I hope you're never late baby."* I was certain something was terribly wrong with me to have to go through all this cock and bullshit. I *was* nervous though; after all, I'd been scheduled to speak with the Institute's intern coordinator, who was a potential supervisor for the first year. I knew this guy and sort of respected him, which made things worse. Also, I felt he thought he knew me. I hated that.

The facade was appropriately dissimilar to all the other polite and formal Boston brownstone buildings on the street. The huge front door opened to a large carpeted entryway, which led to a reception area with a broad winding staircase to the left. It was impressive, not like any mental health center I'd ever seen. No initials carved in the walls. No green tiled decor. The woman at the desk asked my name.

"Anthony," I replied quietly, having never felt comfortable with the name to begin with. I always expected someone to say, "You must be Italian," or some such commentary that made me feel like I should have a box of pizza in my hands and a gun in my pocket. Removing the imaginary sweat-stained Borsalino from my head and red bandanna from my neck, I sat down in the waiting area where the woman gestured for me to go.

"Dr. Rivet will be with you shortly, Mr. Martignetti." She smiled and nodded as she spoke. There was something about her that was both endearing and terrifying. She was like the gatekeeper from Disney Hell. She smilingly opens the door to the infernal abyss, but you only fall a little way and then the princess saves you. Momentarily heartened by the promise of cartoon salvation, I sat in a large leather chair in a reception area that looked, to me, like a Back Bay living room. On the walls and in the glass cases were photographs, framed letters and books, all of it memorabilia of the Institute's founder and his famous friends. It was fancy—like a funeral home. It was much cooler inside the building than outside, but I was still sweating in my pants. This was fertile crotch weather. I was also sure that my hair was both matted and frizzed. Lethal combination. Dirty, insane and ugly. I sat for some time wearing what I imagine was the dog-face.

"Dr. Rivet will see you now." The woman spoke like Bela Lugosi's administrative assistant. *BelalaBelalaBelala-Gosi.* I started turning as if in a dream. I had been visiting the Fortress. I could feel the skin pull back on my face, my eyes torqueing toward her—head moving only slightly. She hadn't gotten up, and I wasn't sure if she was in a wheelchair or not. I acted like she was. I walked to her desk feeling as if my feet were in honey. Playing the old ocular ventriloquist act.

"Where is he please?"

"Fourth floor," she smiled and nodded, her head

bobbing off slowly, never quite still.

"Thank you," my voice as solemn as Henry Kissinger's.

"You're welcome." She nodded and spoke as if we had all the time in the world.

"Excuse me, where is the elevator?"

"There isn't one." She smiled, with a slight increase in her continuous nodding. I was, at this point, furtively checking to see if there were wheels on her chair.

"Oh, okay." I knew that by the time I got to the fourth floor, I'd be so sweat soaked that I'd look alarmingly febrile. I imprudently took the stairs two at a time. Kid was involved. I must have had to borrow his body, since mine was back at the on-ramp with the butterfly. With each few steps I chanted, *"They have pierced my hands and feet, they have numbered all my bones."* As I became winded, I started making "zip-zip-zut-zut-zut" sounds to help me along. These, I imagined, are the kinds of private cluckings psychotics make when they are alone. By the third-floor landing, I became convinced I was developing some kind of narcissistic, paranoid psychosis. A messianic delusion. I'd wind up with the characters in *The Three Christs of Ypsilanti* after the interview. The fourth Christ. The Italian one. Crucified upside down like Mussolini.

I saw a Men's Room sign just off the landing and stopped in to look at myself, catch my breath and dry off.

I was a wreck. Trembling, anxious, stone in my belly, I looked insane. Staring into the mirror, I stretched the dog-face into something more human and said, "What the fuck is wrong with you? You're in paradise compared to the rest of the world. You think you got problems, Mistah? You got nothin' to complain about." Mother Teresa came to mind, with her homeless, naked and starved. Next to her, I was a complete slacker. Though, next to Mama T, everyone is. A contemporary saint. Poor thing. Eventually her head will appear on a Pez dispenser or something. I started getting thought-lost again. The Pez-head idea was a dead giveaway, plus the fact that I started to turn colors from holding my breath. Mama T was beginning to serve as the gateway to the Fortress, I could tell, so I snapped my own head to extricate myself from the mind-jibber, walked out onto the landing and bounded up to the next level. Kid had me in tow.

The fourth floor was the nicest and biggest office I'd ever seen. Joe needed one like this, but he had a mangy corner with three other people. He owned the company, but he looked like a sales clerk. When I would ask him what to put on forms under "Father's Occupation," he would reply, "A clerk, a grocery clerk. That's what I am."

"But Pop, you own the company for chrissake!"

"Hey, Mistah, what are you swearin' for?"

It was almost impossible to have a real conversation with him. Conversation altogether had never been easy. I hoped to become capable of one. Joe always got the short end of everything. His own fault, you could say, but still. Joe was a twin, identical. The kind of twins commonly referred to as "mirror" twins. My uncle was a lefty, Joe, a righty, and they both had the same freckles and marks on their bodies, but on opposite sides. In almost all other ways, they were different. His brother went to college, while Joe stayed and worked the family business. His brother dated and didn't marry until he was 29; Joe married the girl who worked in the donut shop next door when he was 20. He never dated anyone else in his life. His brother drank a little, had a summer home and lived a bit of the good life, while Joe never took a drink and stayed among the clerks. That was Joe. He needed an office like this. He needed a stiff drink and a good fuck is what he needed. Never got either one.

Almost the entire fourth floor of the Danielsen Institute was the office. It had huge bay windows overlooking the Charles River, dark wood, high ceilings— 20 feet or more. There were statuettes of all types around: African fetishes, Hindu goddesses and I even saw a clown. I always hated clowns. *This could be a hard room.* Dr. Rivet swiveled around in his leather desk chair, stood and extended his hand. We shook. My hand was wet, and I only managed to give him about three fingers. I tried to squeeze anyway. It was a kind of desperate, damp claw-hold.

"Carmine Anthony Martignetti." Rivet sat back down and began the conversation for probably the last time. I knew firsthand his reputation for making people uncomfortable. He liked that reputation and pumped it up whenever possible. I said hello. I was really starting to drip all over the place. I must have looked like I just came from ax-murdering my family. I had been scrutinized, inside and out, so closely by my parents that how I look became ridiculously important. The concern never improved my appearance. Rivet sat in silence and looked too much into my eyes. Not that softly fixed gaze, either. This silent stare was Rivet's trademark and way of interacting with students, interns, clients and God knows, probably his closest relationships. He never quite seemed a whole person to me, more like an organ in a jar. A brain suspended in clear liquid in an old university laboratory. I could never get a handle on the guy.

An alarm went off in my pants. It was happening. I figured I had about 30 seconds before I'd start going for my groin. "Eh?" came out of me. I sounded unbelievably like my mother's father. I guess it was meant to be both a question to him and a prediction of panic for me. I was weaving in my seat. Rivet's chin went up, very slightly, in a cryptic response that gave no indication of what he was feeling or thinking. Admittedly, there wasn't much to respond to. He was probably saying to himself, "Oh, of course, another head case who wants to be one of us."

I had to start speaking, to at least distract myself from my groin. Putting the burden of all initial communications on the other person was Rivet's eternal plan.

"I need to know some things about the internship and get some suggestions from you about how best to prepare." Rivet elevated his chin almost imperceptibly and furrowed his brow to accompany a querulous expression. Mussoliniesque.

Il Duce! Il Duce! Il Duce!

"You feel that you need to prepare somehow?" he said. Another long pause. All of Italy waited, sweating.

"Eh?" I was speaking as Jackie's father again. No apparent response came from Rivet. Who could blame him?

"Well, you know, what can I do to get ready for this internship?" I was anticipating a tangle ahead.

"What you bring doesn't seem to be enough—perhaps you sense that you lack something, and you want me to tell you what that is?" Rivet was all seriousness.

Holy Jesus, I thought, what's with this guy, does he have normal conversations or what the fuck? I could tell that I was beginning to look as though I'd contracted jungle fever.

"I don't know about all that—I just mean do you want to tell me something about the internship that I should know before I begin?"

"Do you want me to say anything in particular that may be of help?" He was fucking intractable.

Better to live one day as a lion than 100 years as a lamb.
Il Duce, Il Duce, Il Duce!!

"Look, I'm somewhat nervous about beginning; it's hard for me to feel like I really fit in, and so I'm a little anxious about it." I thought that might have been the wrong thing to say. I started feeling slightly disoriented, since my brain was cogitating on what I had just said, what he might say and what I'd say in response, all at the same time.

Rivet, having heard the words *nervous* and *anxious*, sensed emotion leaking into the room and wanted to swim in for a bite. He began peering directly at the wall to his left, supporting his chin with his fist. *Duce! Duce! Duce!* I felt tempted to sneak a glance at the wall, too, as if I'd find Rivet's cue cards hung there, or perhaps the Rome train schedule.

He looked back at me and said, "You're nervous about not fitting in; you don't feel as if there is a place for you here that is safe or comfortable yet." It's like he had been a fun-house mirror in a former life.

"That may be one way to say it." I didn't want to let too many words in that weren't my own. He didn't know me and couldn't be allowed to speak for me. "Safe" and "comfortable" sounded a bit twinkie for my appetite. I had to begin to mark my territory. I'm no *Panetista[1]*. If not one day as a lion, at least I'd have 50 years as a dog.

"Uh-huh." Rivet thoughtfully considered the distinction I had made. "I'm confused; you fooled me," he said, chin up, brow furrowed. "It was my experience, at least based on my observation of you over the last few years, that you had found a way to make this program and the people in it feel like home for you."

I wondered if I was being criticized, or if he was laying some kind of a trap for me. He might have been accusing me of being a fraud. I always worried about possible arrest by the fraud police.

"I'm just telling you how I feel right now. I mean, I'm not as dislocated as I was back then, but I still feel that way somewhat."

"And you're telling me this because . . .?" Rivet lifted his head. He was ready to catch my reply in his mouth. The pause was too much. I looked over at the cue card. Unbelievably, Rivet broke his own silence.

"Perhaps to bring me on board with how you're

---

[1] Joe used to use this term to refer to Italian foot soldiers, who would fight for whichever side fed them.

feeling? And that may be reason enough, Anthony."

"Yes, I guess that's why I'm telling you." It's lucky he made some attempt. I was getting ready to insert one of those statuettes into his throat.

"And why me specifically?" Rivet added.

For the love of God, will this never end? Why beat the thing to death? Why can't we just have a normal conversation? I was into a full head-babble, all the while trying to be unnoticed in my constant squirming to get some crotch relief. I thought, let Kid do it, the hell with it.

"Ah . . . because I trust . . . ah . . . I trust . . . the process." These, the young one knew to be good buzzwords.

"The process?" asked Rivet, shining his mirror-self with a dust cloth.

"Well, actually, I guess I probably have come to trust *you* somewhat, you know, through the program and all." I felt incredibly weak right then, having said that. I almost went to the Fortress again. I could tell. I was feeling the beginning of a rectal prolapse. My mouth opened, dog-faced, lower lip as pendulous as a water balloon.

"Well, Anthony, consider me on board."

His words almost frightened me. I was awake and breathing, but I could have fallen asleep right then. Kid threw a couple of shots, then left me with the rest of the round. *Bing-bang-boom* "*I'm outta here!*" Freakin' clown.

"Okay, thanks." I was exhausted from having been heard.

"Anthony, when people come here, they often revert to earlier levels of adaptation. They regress, in part, due to the intensity of the schedule, the scrutiny they are under and the fact that the work is demanding and important. Everyone goes through it, even the staff. You are here because you were chosen to be here. You should, as you suggested, trust the process. We expect people to move beyond their current levels of understanding and development—that's all we expect, only that they expand beyond the place they are emotionally when they enter."

Rivet stopped just in time. I caught every word. I can easily tune out in the face of too many words, because I had my listening overused as a kid by people who had no ears. Joe was a continuous violator of Ockham's razor. He multiplied explanations beyond all necessity.

Mr. Huge, for example, would sit in tense silence for hours, looking like he was going to combust, and then he'd talk you stupid. He wavered between somewhat animated yet guarded enthusiasm, and a slow burn based in fear and self-loathing, which he projected onto all of us. Joe, in summer, lumbered around the house in enormous white boxer shorts, carrying a 9 iron, wearing a very serious face. If you weren't used to him, you'd think he was going to kill somebody. In winter, he'd sit around after work with his office clothes on, undershirt, dress shirt and necktie all tucked into his boxer shorts, the elastic waistband of which was riding two inches above his pants.

He'd reach behind, hold the back of his neck and, with a mildly annoyed and querulous expression, call out, "Jackie, Jackie!"

"What is it, Joe?" Jackie would respond with an ever-present irritation in her voice.

"Is something open?" he'd ask, sounding like a little kid.

"What do you mean, open?"

"I feel a draft."

"Nothing is open, Joe."

"Are you sure?"

"Yes, Joe, it's the middle of January. Nothing is open."

"But I feel a draft on the back of my head."

"I'd know if something was open. It's all in your head."

He'd then drift off into television and skull-chatter la-la land from where he had come, mumbling, "My head, huh? *My* head, she says. That's what I'm talkin' about, my head."

Jesus, who's that . . . Chip? I thought. I had started thinking along his lines. Brainwashed. Chip was definitely making an appearance, analyzing all the family shit and its effect on me. I didn't want to carry him around inside, but Chip, that little fuck, persisted.

The talk with Rivet was easier than I thought it would be. Partial understanding, mild encouragement— what's the big deal? It took a while to get there with the likes of Rivet, but at least it wasn't totally cold at both ends of the pool.

"Okay." I started to wake. "Do you have a book or two you would suggest for the next few weeks?" I felt clean in the question.

"How about Alice Miller's *The Drama of the Gifted Child*," Rivet offered quickly. "Have you read it?"

"No." I was suspicious about how particularly this book might apply to me. "What's it about?"

"The effect of early life experiences of non-empathic responses by parents, and how children react in creative ways to try to feel loved and human. Some of the reasons children develop compensatory structures." Again, I caught every word. Rivet spoke as if what he said was very important, not only to me, but to himself and everyone else.

"Compensatory structures," I reiterated.

"Yes, Anthony, the attempts people make to develop a sense of self when there is a feeling that the self is not sufficiently supported by significant others in the person's life—when there are narcissistic injuries." He said these words and held my gaze as if seeking even the tiniest reaction. I gave him none, only the frozen expression and suspended breath I had to endure for 20 seconds while he watched.

"Great, thanks." I said exhaling, and got up. Rivet followed. I offered my hand; Rivet took it—all four fingers and thumb were involved.

"See you in about a month," he said.

"Yes, thanks again." I immediately felt that I gave thanks too often.

Leaving the office, I was slightly unsteady on my feet, but secure enough to negotiate the four flights and attempt an interaction with the woman in the reception area. Kid had already left the building and was probably leaning against the Jeep.

The receptionist looked up as I descended from the landing. She bobbed her head with a half smile and said, "Very good, Mr. Martignetti."

I looked for her nameplate. "Thank you, Ms. Kiley," I replied, not knowing what was very good. "And please call me Anthony."

"Very good, Anthony." She said it again. "You may call me Annette. We shall be seeing a lot more of you soon, I expect."

"Yes, thank you." I couldn't stop myself from saying thank you; it was ridiculous. I backed my way out of the reception area to Annette's continuous nodding and smiling.

I stepped out onto Bay State Road, got in the Jeep and drove home. No music. I sang "Rocky Raccoon" over and over between a little thinking. *"Somewhere in the black mountain hills of Dakota there lived a young boy named Rocky Raccoon, ah . . ."*

I thought that maybe things wouldn't be so bad. I remembered times over the years, even up to the end, talking to Joe and having a good conversation. I used to feel loose inside. I could face the world. Even others in the family would agree there was nothing like having a good talk with him. A good talk was little more than coming away, sometimes from the phone, feeling one-quarter heard, not criticized or insulted, and even mildly encouraged and supported—all in fewer than 5,000 words. I cherished those rarities.

The Beatles were still playing in my head as I sat parked near my apartment. *"She and her man, who called himself Dan, were in the next room at the hoedown . . ."* My voice was indistinguishable from a Brit's. I could do any accent and many voices. One time when my grand-mother's voice came out in a therapy session, Chip said, "How many people are in there anyway?"

"Eh," I responded, while shrugging my shoulders and smiling. This, I think, was my way of saying "I have no response for you." "Eh" was the only sound I ever made that was Jackie's father. He was a quiet man.

As for me, I could always act out people, voices and parts. This was a source of both pride and fear. I was happy I could create something with mood, body and sound, but I feared that I couldn't distinguish between acting and living authentically as myself. I mentioned that I was ripe for fraudulence accusations. I always felt a kind of moat between me and my experiences. It's the "seeming to go away for a minute" petit mal thing. Chip knew about it. It was a sort of insulation. In some ways, I couldn't imagine life without it. It was like water to a fish. It was where I lived.

I never liked being called a fake. Few people ever accused me in earnest, or so I chose to believe. I had been safe, at least, from that level of confrontation. I was glad Rivet wasn't more direct about it. If he were, it's questionable what my reaction would have been. I was afraid of caving in like a political prisoner in the Gulag. *Confess, you rat; confess that you are a fraud.*

"Fuck you, you asshole" wouldn't have really cut it with Rivet. I still thought that maybe Rivet had made a veiled suggestion about my inauthenticity when he said, "You fooled me," and then tried to weasel out of it.

Back in the apartment, things seemed okay. Rivet was on board, and life felt like a good conversation with Joe. I decided that I wanted to read and swim for the four weeks before the fellowship started. Read, swim and ride my bike, actually. Actually, read, swim, ride my bike, drink, flirt, feel and be admired by all who met me. Yes, this was the plan, eternally. I knew, though, that I would settle for simply avoiding injury over the next month. Maybe I would start meditating again. Drag out the old picture of my guru, light a little incense . . . go for my groin. I remembered the question I asked Rivet; maybe I was still trying to find an answer. Rivet mentioned my thinking that I lacked something for the internship and needed to prepare myself in some way. I was afraid that he might have been onto something.

"Maybe," I said to myself, "just maybe I'll do nothing. Maybe I'll just waste time. Enormous wasting of time." This, I knew, was perfect. I would do nothing to prepare. Get up whenever the hell I felt like it, crash around the apartment with no plan, piss, eat, sleep again if I wanted to, listen to the radio, drink whiskey in the morning, smoke if I liked. French cigarettes, real lung busters. Grow a beard, such as it is, read *People* magazine, watch *Oprah*. I could talk on the phone all day, or not at all. I felt wonderfully groggy already. I could be late for everything. I remembered my song an hour earlier, outside the Danielsen. I began to chant, "*Always* late, *always* late baby, I hope you're *always* late."

I immediately thought of Joe's reaction to this plan. If he could, he'd vault out of the mausoleum just to register, in grand fashion and with no holds barred, his total disgust with my preparatory strategy and with people like me. "Not even with *me*," I said out loud, "but with people *like* me." I would become an abstract and dehumanized member of a group of miscreants and therefore disqualified as a mirror reflection for Joe: *His Majesty the Infant,* kicking around in his gigantic diapers. King Baby. I wondered how I had become so agitated. I had only been thinking of what to do with the next four weeks. And already I was preparing for a life and death battle with the decomposed body of my long-dead father.

"Buried alive," I said and whipped around like Edgar Allan Poe was standing behind me next to Rod Serling. I had some growing to do—that was clear.

The days passed hotter and lazier. I worked less than 10 hours a week at a hospital in Concord, seeing patients who were both substance abusers and suffering from a definable mental disorder. Twice a week I counseled three dual-diagnosis patients and did an occasional intake report with a newly admitted person. I had worked in this field years earlier, after completing my master's. This, coupled with the five years of course work for the doctorate, made the job feel manageable, and it went smoothly. I didn't even have to wear a tie, just be there and listen, try to understand, and attempt to explain my understanding.

This process, if it was even close to the mark, seemed the key to cure in therapy. I had little idea of why it worked; I knew some of how. Probably something about Rivet's notion of compensatory structures. I wondered about Chip—was he as lost in the process as I sometimes felt? The thought sent a shudder through my neck. If Chip didn't know what was going on with me, then maybe I was really just out there. *Naw.*

"Well, fuck Chip," I said out loud, then immediately thought I was having an unconscious reaction to whomever Chip was supposed to represent for me. Jesus. "Maybe I'm really angry; maybe I have reason to be." Maybe Chip had been right to be pushing into all those *abuse* issues, as he insisted upon referring to them. Maybe it had something to do with what I thought I lacked for the internship that Rivet was talking about. I thought, *Well, fuck Chip anyway.* Jesus, he was starting to annoy me.

When disturbing thoughts surfaced, I used to try to relax and recall a feeling of being connected to myself and others. One with *e v e r y t h i n g.* The guru tried to teach me this. I assumed the half lotus position, which seemed as natural as ever at first. I lasted seven torturous minutes.

"Christ Jesus," I said, wondering briefly about the meaning of my continual invocation of the divine. I knew a guy, a patient at the hospital in Concord, who was into a full-blown anxiety disorder with panic attacks. As part of his treatment, he was sitting in meditation for

30 minutes, twice a day. I felt that mine had been at least a 20-minute sit. Seven minutes. I shook my watch, stared at it, shook it some more and stared at it again, felt exhausted and rolled off the cushion onto my back.

"Eh," I uttered. I lay there in static doom.

"People don't change," I said. "Not really, they just fool themselves. Only the channels change: NBC–ABC–CBS–Cable." I flirted with the idea of declining the fellowship and joining a monastery. "Monk," I said, eyes tilted toward the ceiling. I remembered a quote by Ben Franklin: "The eyes of other people are the eyes that ruin us. If all but myself were blind, I should want neither fine clothes, fine houses nor fine furniture." This, I had always felt to be true. I occasionally wondered why others' eyes are not the ones that preserve and sustain us. Perhaps in another universe.

I was actually afraid to be a shrink—always had been— to engage in the process of face-to-face mutual human trauma healing. Afraid of living and dying. Always wondering if I'd have regrets. Thinking I was creating my future regrets now. This was all normal. This was life as I had been told it would be and seen it to be. Life as I expected it to be. Life in the stinking fish tank.

Morning brought the 9th of September. Seven a.m., awakened by alarm. I felt excited about what was ahead of me—excited and, I was vaguely noticing, somewhat not there. The orientation conference, held on a beautiful country estate, would give me an opportunity to encounter the other 13 interns. Thinking about meeting them had me wavering between grandiosity and insignificance. Me: champion and dung beetle. We would gather for the first time at the Danielsen and be shuttled an hour northwest, to university-owned property. I stared long and hard in the mirror. I seemed puffy. I wanted to look just right, especially today.

After a shower I cleared a bit. I gagged while brushing my teeth. I always brushed deeply into my throat, having never in my life, even once, been sure about my breath. I opted for slightly overformal clothes, the whole time feeling as if I were wearing a *Made in Italy* sign on my lapel. I made a special effort to show no bulges in my pockets. I've always hated that.

"Lean, mean, smooth as silk," I said. I began to throw a few uppercuts and hooks, "lean and mean, lean and mean." I started to sweat immediately. It was a muggy morning. I wondered why I was always doing these stupid things and wrecking myself. "Sweat-head." I left the apartment, climbed into the Jeep and drove toward Route 2. I passed the butterfly death scene at the on-ramp and reflected for a moment about life and its passing.

On the road I fussed with some tapes. I was between choosing Tom Waits and Lead Belly, but opted instead for the Domingo, Carreras and Pavarotti concert my brother Michael ordered for me from PBS. Over and over I listened to Pavarotti sing *"Recondita armonia"*—this was an aria Joe used to try to sing me as a boy. By the time I reached the Coliseum at Harvard, the music took hold. I burst out in tears. I had been trying to do this. Kind of playing with myself again. I cried for my father and for his father. I cried for myself, for what I had loved, lost and for what I never had. I cried and cried for nothing and no one. I cried for Mother Teresa, for Tom Waits, for Jackie and even Chip, but most of all, I cried for Joe. My silk tie became wrinkled and spotted with tears falling from my nose and chin. I wiped my face with it. I didn't care about who might see me all in bits on the road as they passed in morning traffic. I moaned and yelled all the way to the Institute, and practically threw up at one point.

I parked on Bay State Road a little late and tried to collect myself. I knew my eyes were red and swollen, my tie, stained, damp and twisted. I didn't need to consult the mirror to know how I looked. I was as wet and raw as an infant and felt like I had popped out of a cocoon too early. I walked into the building and Annette met me. "Good morning, Mr. Martignetti . . . I mean Anthony."

"Good morning, Annette," I said, sounding as if my head was filled with saltwater.

"You look very nice today," she added.

"Thank you."

"The others are in the staff lounge upstairs; they have been expecting you."

"Very good Annette, and thank you," I said, and took the stairs as they came.

That was then. I completed the training, wrote my dissertation and published my research—quite a story in itself—and became a shrink, full-fledged.

It's a different world, and I'm a different man. Kid, he's not in the picture as much. Most of the others are gone too, sitting quietly in the shadows of each day. It's mainly just me now, Doctor M.

Call me if you want; I'm in the book. We'll see what we can do for you.

The end.

Though stories are never really finished; they just stop . . . like most lives . . . never done, only over.

Mad

I've known a lot of crazy women. Always liked them best; actresses, musicians, freaks, artists, prostitutes, ones who, as it turned out, had multiple personalities, girls with problems, girls in situations. The ones you'd practically have to unstrap from their straight jackets just so they could smoke a joint. The crazier they were, the more I liked them.

Of all of them, Madrigal might have been the craziest, and her angle on life was crazy in the best sense of the word. I called her Mad.

We met in 1966. She was in her pre-hippie phase, a painter, who played wooden flutes of various kinds, which she called her "love sticks." She smoked pot whenever she could, and tripped on acid, mushrooms and mescaline. Hardly seemed to eat, except for fruits and salads. She was tall and skinny with waist-length hair. She was willowy and witchy and enchantingly free. She was mostly happy and sometimes cried when she was, and when she cried, her face was wide open and luminous, like a tenor hitting the highest note in an aria. She could also be tragic, mystical and dark, and loved running around under the night moon as much as she did in sunshine. She burned incense all the time and smelled of exotic oils and musky sweat. She had an odd array of intriguing physical attributes, which attracted me as well, including beautiful eyes and hands, legs and feet . . . and a voice . . . a voice, which could launch a thousand erections. Not to mention her hair, itself a point of fascination for most people who met her, and which she once sold a chunk of to wig makers. And she could use each of these attributes, along with countless others, in various combinations to please, torment and mystify.

She had sandals you'd imagine Mary Magdalene would have worn, which she seldom had on, and often carried dangling off her index finger, even when it was chilly outside. In colder weather she'd ditch the sandals and wear mukluks she bought in Nova Scotia. She had a huge cloth satchel on a long strap with Indian designs that hung from her shoulder to her knee, where she kept her flutes, fruits and countless prized and enchanted possessions. All her clothes danced—flowing like water around her. She was the most alive person I'd ever known. With her I felt plugged into a socket. It seemed to me she would always be just young.

She'd say wicked and what sounded like nonsensical things right into my ear. She'd get in my face nose-to-nose, forehead-to-forehead, eyeball-to-eyeball, and speak in a weird raspy voice like a devil was talking. She said her eyes were like x-rays that could see deep into me. And, except for her occasional proclamations, demonic, demented sounding or not, she was most often silent, and quite still, even in all her motion.

She loved "Ode on a Grecian Urn" by Keats. She said the poem was about us, and all the truth and beauty, which we had converted into flesh. She said the poem was hers and not Keats's, and that meant she had full entitlement to declare what it was about. And I believed her, and that she was that "unravished bride of quietness," the "foster-child of Silence and slow Time." I even think the poem had something to do with why she played the "pipes."

She. Was. Crazy. She was fluent in Spanish and once in a while I called her Loco. But somehow, in the midst of it all, she made sense.

She held my head on her long thighs for hours in the woods while we read, recited or made up poetry. She liked Byron and, of course, Keats; I preferred the Beat and Hispanic poets. We lived in a fantasy of beauty and perversion. We figured we were great at understanding the universe, and conjuring up profound and remote thoughts . . . making a meal of our time together, and sex and drugs were always on the menu.

Her attention to me knew no bounds. I'd get a hard-on just showering or getting into my jeans when I knew I was going to see her. In those moments of anticipation, everything felt and smelled crisp, including my own skin. It seemed springtime would go on end-lessly. I was as crazy as she was, maybe. I was . . . *into her*. I was scared of her too, because I loved her in the only way I could love then and be so young and stoned. It was, for me, a shaky feeling, as if her mad attention could crack my bones and my world wide open.

We were together four years, more or less. We met when I was 17, and she was a year younger. It was always off and on with us, months here and there, followed by sometimes long breaks. During our time we shared a lot of experiences, especially sexual ones, and they were electrifying and varied. She'd put her tongue in my ass and slide it in and out. That was mostly when we did speed. The first time she did that to me, I was naked on my belly on a brown shag carpet and shot off into the long strands like a fire hose in a forest.

She twice traveled to stay with me when I lived outside the U.S. Once she was on her hands and knees at my apartment in Canada, while I sat on her, using her long hair as reins. I was just fooling around . . . playing horsey. It was fun, and then I got the idea to masturbate and squirted, lickety-split, on her back and in her hair. She got angry with me, which she almost never did. She said because she didn't know I was beating off up there, and it would have been okay if I'd told her. I understood . . . she always wanted to be in charge of, or at least involved in, anything like that.

She whacked me off a number of times with her beautiful, flexible feet. Sometimes they were grass-stained or black with the earth, and I think I liked that even better. She was alive, the way the earth was, and always linked with it. She took great pleasure in having control of anything coming out of my dick. Always wanted to hold it when I was pissing. She liked aiming and directing the stream around. Back then I was capable of producing great slashings of piss, and she'd be able to write my initials in the snow. Said she liked the feeling under the shaft when the pee was coming through, and would hold her fingertips there like she was taking a pulse.

She loved playing with my cock and hung on to it like it was the Holy Cross, as if she had Jesus by the balls, as if she had the power to make a miracle occur in torn blue jeans. For her, getting my cock out of my pants was the equivalent of getting King Arthur's Excalibur out of the stone. Granted, this sword was effortless to liberate, but she regarded it as a triumph each time. There were occasions where she had my dick all propped up in her hands while I was lying there, and she'd play at making it rise and fall, shrink and grow with her words and voice and sometimes the music from her instrument. She'd turn my cock into a kind of flute-charmed serpent. It seemed she felt she had the world in her hands and could get the whole thing to spin on the head of my penis.

For her, my dick was a representation, perhaps in the way an Indian lingam is, and when we were together, she was Shakti and I was Shiva. I began to see my penis as something different from my body. It's as if I went full circle and became a phallic symbol even to myself. Seems she just wanted to possess it. We discussed Freud's penis-envy theories and she said she had no such envy, because she had the use of mine and she was happy with that. She liked being in control of bodies, animating them, enjoying them; bodies, like the earth itself, represented what was most real for her. She was not, as the bumper sticker now asserts, *"a spiritual being having a human experience"*; anything that could have been referred to as "spiritual" was, for Mad, an accidental finding. She was embodied. Fully. Mad was life.

From me, she never wanted too much in the way of sexual attention. I only ever was inside her three times. She enjoyed kissing me, and liked me to lick her breasts and legs sometimes, and I would whenever she wanted. But she was hell-bent on getting me to cum, and I was happy with that.

She'd blow me up and down like she was playing that flute of hers. She blew me at parties in other people's bathrooms, and in the old Mercury while I was driving—speeding down the highway, shrieking in ecstasy. Usually, I'd tap her on the cheek just before I'd cum, because she said she didn't want it to "cry" in her mouth, except when I was driving . . . then it was okay, because there was no good place for me to go with it without endangering everyone. She referred to blowjobs as "rain," and was always telling me, *"It looks like rain"* as a code when other people were around. Or she'd ask me what the weather looked like while drilling me with a Mona Lisa smile that only I could detect. My cock would jump in my jeans whenever she mentioned the weather; even if it was the weather she was talking about.

Man she could suck; she was all lips and tongue and as if she didn't have a tooth in her mouth. She'd go part way down the shaft, swirling her tongue around the head of my penis the way her dresses danced around those immaculate legs. Mad never hurt me, and rain always washed us clean. She'd work me with her hands in movie theaters and with her feet under tables in diners, where I'd cum in my pants, beaming and smirking at her like a mute fool right in front of my meatloaf special.

One time I contemplated getting the word "rain" tattooed between my bellybutton and my cock, with the sun and moon on either side, but never did. I got another one down there instead, one that doesn't speak of life. I pretty much gave up on getting blowjobs after Mad and I went our own ways. Nobody could do it to her level or my satisfaction. Compared to Mad, most other girls seemed to have brains like peanuts, mouths like wood chippers, and ignorant, inflexible legs. I never trusted anyone's mouth so much as I did hers, both what came out of it and what went in.

She was crazy, but as I said, she made sense, at least to me.

She said she never wanted to crucify a lifetime with crossword puzzles or macramé.

She said everything was nothing and it would always be that way.

She said the pursuit of happiness was an American joke.

She told me that the first time she tripped, she knew there was no God, because she saw him and he was a baby and a loser who should've already found everyone by now.

She said life should be given full expression every day, and the way to that was through kissing, music, art, drugs and getting me to cum.

She said I'd do well to hide my tongue in my mouth, or she'd take it out to keep for herself and rub it over her body whenever she wanted, and I wouldn't be able to say a word about it.

She said she liked what I said and the way I said things, but thought it had a lot to do with my mouth.

She said I was the best boy she ever kissed.

She said it was wrong to honor a concept ahead of a human being.

She said that people should make art, and that art should never be a race to anywhere, not a goal to be attained, but done only for its own sake.

She said that her body was an instrument of peace, and that she wanted me to be a piece of her instrument.

She said she'd like to shrink me down with her x-ray eyes so I could fit in her flute and live in her satchel; this way she could take me out and blow me whenever she wanted.

She said she loved me.

I told her the same. But it always made me nervous.

Mad was special. She was. And the word genius would not be wasted on a description of her. But, as the ancients professed, genius comes for a visit, then goes. And so it was with Mad.

We'd all but lost touch for a long while, only a call or a letter now and then, till I was 30. That was the third time I was inside her. She showed up at my apartment one night—50 miles from where she lived—with a guy she was engaged to, who looked like a nightly reject from Studio 54. He had a weird haircut and wore a white linen suit like he was auditioning to be an extra on *Miami Vice.* He was a pallid, tepid buffoon, as far as I could tell. That night I was with a girl I'd later marry and divorce. Even with the four of us there, Mad tortured me mercilessly across the living room of my small apartment, communicating with me in ways only she could, popping her foot in and out of her dangling high heel and liquefying me with her wicked gaze. The mullet-sporting fiancé, who got drunk and passed out on my couch, didn't notice her evil antics, and my girlfriend didn't either.

Mad could hide in plain view and speak to me in secret like no other. It would take a windtalker to break her codes. (Not long after, she broke up with the buffoon. When I heard that, it restored my confidence in her. She'd been wearing a fat diamond on her perfect hand, and was more stylish and refined in her appearance, but she was still Mad.)

After that night we were crazy to be together, phoning and sneaking around to meet. We went to the movies to see the French film *Get Out Your Handker-chiefs*. She rubbed my dick so artfully through my pants in the theater that I was groaning for half the film, and though she kept putting her hand over my mouth, she never let up on me. Once I'd climaxed, she reached into her bag and, in her slow and silent way, got out a hankie and dangled it in my face. She thought that was funny, given the movie title. Afterwards we returned to my apartment and banged like Dirt Devils. She didn't want to get high; said she'd started having panic attacks when she smoked weed some years back and wouldn't risk it again. It was a little weird that third time inside her; we were changing and had changed and, for me, the world began to deflate.

Our communications following that night became sporadic and rare. She visited me a few times, when I was about 40, at an office I had in Wellesley, after I was married for the second time. She'd informed me when she got married, told me when she had a daughter and then when she had a son, she told me when her father passed away, and finally came to see me after her mother died. On that visit the changes were even more conspicuous. Seemed she might have been on some pills, not the type we used to swallow, not the living ones, but the ones that take the life out of you . . . the dying pills.

I didn't know much about the man she married, but from what I gathered, she couldn't relate to his mind. She had changed her last name, and the way she looked, and had cut her hair to a quarter of its original length. She was still breast-feeding both of her kids; the oldest had long passed her fifth birthday. A couple of times she brought the two of them to my office, where I'd stare at them and then they'd play for a while with my secretary, Carlita, while Mad and I talked. The oldest one kept trying to get her head under her mother's long shirt, saying, *"Momma, c'mon—c'mon, I want to . . . your nunnies are like juice packs."*

Seemed Mad still liked having jurisdiction over bodies.

Her husband was very insecure, and jealous, and was in the habit of tracking her odometer to keep tabs on her whereabouts. He found she was occasionally logging more miles in a day than she should have been. He'd only ever heard about me from times gone by, but one day he acted on a hunch, and looked me up in the phone book to see if I was listed in the area. He discovered that I was and made a call to my office, and when my secretary answered, he asked for her name. Sure enough, Mad had told him she'd been occasionally visiting a friend named Carlita, and at the moment of hearing her name, he knew for sure she'd been seeing me. Then, all hell broke loose for Mad. He demanded that she never contact me again and threatened to leave her and take the kids if she did.

She came the next week, anxious and a little more robotic. It was a rainy summer afternoon; she was wearing a black, shiny slicker that reached almost to the ground and gold-colored ballet flats. She wore extra makeup on her eyes and bright pink lipstick. She kicked off her shoes and put her bare feet up on my desk; they were perfectly clean and her toes were painted a sparkly gold. As soon as she did that, she threw open her slicker, under which she wore a summery dress that buttoned from her breasts to her ankles but was undone from the bottom to the top of her thighs, revealing the extent of her long, tanned legs. I think she knew it was a parting shot she was giving me.

I had a globe in my office; it was actually a beach ball with the countries and major cities on it as the design. She asked me to hand it to her, and toyed with it while we spoke. When it was time for her to go, she flipped open the plug and slowly squeezed the air out until the globe was flat, and then flopped it on my desk. That was the last of it . . . an anxious call or two from her the following month, but nothing else for 25 years since.

She had become human in the worst possible meaning of it. She shrank into life. It was the greatest example I'd ever had that death is real. She, the mad one . . . she, who was always and only young . . . fell under the deflated world . . . the weight of years . . . money, marriage, children, and cocks gone old and cold.

I imagine that by now, if she's not dead, she's as good as dead. Dead as Keats. I think about trying to find her once in a while, but she's gone. Maybe she's gone the way I am. I must be gone off somewhere, because I can't feel the grass, the summer, the sea, my jeans or shirt or her legs in my body anymore. I cannot feel the languid youth, which was once mine and hers. That is gone. But I know, even if I found her, she'd never admit that anything's gone, and through her creased mouth, and from her blue eyes, surrounded by aging flesh, she'd do her voice and be her way, assuring me I was still alive in here.

So, given present circumstances, I will have to speak for Mad, to reanimate her, to appropriate her, leaving her to be that "bride of quietness." And in her newest incarnation, she would tell me that *all of apparent life comes to the same end . . . apparent death, but that these are only apparent and, therefore, illusions.* And just as Mad appropriated bodies, she appropriated Keats's poem. She embodied the Ode. She would say that *she and I are timeless, eternal, and that we live on that ancient Grecian urn.* She would remind me that *the leaves of the tree on that urn will never fade and it will always be spring, and that we live between the past and the future in the eternal now. And the now,* she would say, *is only and always mad.* And then, because she was a shape-shifter . . . the mad one would emerge from the depths of age and, right before my eyes, into blooming young life once again, moving toward me and hungry for fun.

But that's just another distorted fantasy, because, though Mad was life, mad-life is no more.

Now life is normal, which means dying, and dead. Dead normal. It's as if I've been hit in the face with a board every day for so long that now I just wait for it. I wait for it after I wake, or when it's late at night and I'm alone. I lie on my couch some nights imagining my head in her lap, or her feet in mine. I wait, imagining, but nothing comes, and nothing is fresh, not jeans, or shirt . . . not summer . . . or music . . . not flesh . . . and no Madrigal . . .

For ever piping songs for ever new . . . When old age shall this generation waste, thou shalt remain, in midst of other woe than ours, a friend to man, to whom thou say'st, 'Beauty is truth, truth beauty,—that is all ye know on earth, and all ye need to know.'

Dog: *A Meditation on Love*

I don't know what makes me think I love my dog. I've felt something like love for him, and imagined that he loves me—but he doesn't and I can tell. Poochy seems to love my wife more than he does me, but that's not true either. He loves us the same, which comes down to—not so much. And if he doesn't love me, how've I've fooled myself into thinking I love him? Love has to be a two-way affair. Otherwise it's just delusion, right?

Now, when I say he doesn't love me, what I mean is, he doesn't love me in a personal way. He's like a baby. Babies don't know ships from Toyotas—breasts from baby bunting—they'll suck off of anything and anybody—a nurse, a nanny, a man, a wolf, a monkey. Babies don't love you. I don't mean to be love's assassin here, but they don't. Later on they can love the hell out of you and that might be the best thing in the world. But babies, loving you for real? *Nnnnn*, sorry. And dogs are like babies who never grow up.

Dogs will hump anything too—males, females, people's legs, their toys, their beds. My dog's been trying to get busy with his bed since he first laid eyes on it. It was hump at first sight. And likewise, his love act toward me has nothing whatsoever to do with *who I am*. He loves me as I love nature—or lobster—or wine. I love each lobster and each glass of wine as it comes to me. I love nature in each day and in each circumstance I find it. I love these things when I'm actually involved with them, and then I forget them while moving on to the next experience. I am not attached to them; I am not faithful to them. And yet, somehow, I feel a kind of love for and from my dog despite certain knowledge of his utter emotional infidelity. I am a meal ticket, end of story. But I'll continue.

My dog loves food. He'd jump into Idi Amin's mouth if he sensed there was a morsel of meat lodged between the guy's teeth. He'd play Saddam Hussein's staunch ally for stale crumbs of pita bread. He'd dive off a rocky cliff, in front of a herd of lemmings, just to get at an empty Dunkin' Donuts bag. He'd sell me down river for a Tic Tac. I know this, just the way I know that tomorrow never comes.

Aside from his status as a sentient being (toward

which I, being a Buddhist-type, am obligated to emanate compassion), he is, first and foremost, an artist. Now here, I mean a con artist. Con-artistry is a complicated form of art with a long history and many masters. And I, in a grudging sort of way, respect my dog for it. He is dedicated—single-minded about his calling—and sacrifices all for his art. You gotta respect that. Since respect is an important component of love, perhaps I've confused that particular ingredient with the entire recipe.

Now, the term con artist does not refer, as many believe, to "con" as in x-con—convict; no, it refers to confidence. A con man is one who takes you into his confidence, and in so doing creates the impression that he is your friend (which he is not), cares about you (which he does not), and makes himself vulnerable to you sometimes at great peril to himself (which is patently untrue). This is a skill which has afforded countless men the uneasy enjoyment of viewing their profiles on *America's Most Wanted* for having bilked trusting women out of their pensions, inheritances and heirlooms. Novice con men will go for the short change and feign risking arrest to buy you marijuana with your hard-earned cash, but go to the movies instead while you wait for hours in the rain unwilling to admit what a chump you are. The thing about cons is that they take you and you can't believe it until it's too late—and it's this very disbelief which affords them their much-needed getaway time.

Now my dog is an *evolutionary* con artist; it's just the way his species developed, all of them derivatives of the wolf. Being a con was not his idea; he doesn't have any big ideas, only little ones. As I said, he's like a baby—he wants his mother, or any handy replacement. Essentially, he's a wolf pup wrapped in baby blankets. Even better, he's a lamb in sheep's clothing. I say his artistry is evolutionary because, think about it—what other animal in the history of civilization has figured out a way to be the genuine friend of humankind?

You may offer the cat as an option—but no—cats can't be counted as genuine friends. (Your cat does not love you in a personal way. If it seems to, that's just because it is mentally ill.) They are more like visitors from another planet that we are not particularly afraid of, and whom we tolerate among us. Cats, all the while, believe that *we* are the extraterrestrials—shuttled in just to look after them. Cats. Not genuine friends as far as I can tell and I've looked after a number of them.

A cat will shred your furniture, and your flesh, glare at you anytime it gets a mind to, bring woodland creatures into the kitchen that have been half-gutted and dragged in by their remaining entrails, constantly molt dander-laden fur on your now shredded furnishings, refuse to come when called, and God forbid if you don't tend to the stink-box of a toilet they require, they will turn your home into a dung-littered ammonia depository.

And for all this, a cat will use you as a lounge cushion or a kneading platform when it feels like it and you're so happy for what you get you make it into a big hoopla. "*Oooooh* look at kitty, hun, isn't she wonderful? She loves her mommy, don't you Muffy? Oh-what-a-good-girl."

Cat looks up at you: "*Muffy? Vhat are you meshuganeh? Clean the stink-box or I'll pee on the fridge again. Oy vey, these aliens.*" At least with cats, you know where you stand. You know right well they don't give a rat's anus about you and you accept it (that is, unless you buy into the mentally ill ones out of guilt because you made them that way).

But a dog is a con. My dog, anyway—but I think all dogs—and they, from breakfast till bedtime, are busy selling you the Brooklyn Bridge of love and affection. Still, I become his bitch whenever he softens his eyes in a love trance because I have something he wants, and with one paw pitifully raised, basically speaks: "I love you—*love—love—love* you, just as you are. Never seen anything like you. You're my *e-v-e-r-y-t-h-i-n-g*. Have pity on poor me . . . help the needy." He practically breaks into song: "*I, I who have nothing, I, I who have no one, adore you and want you so. I'm just a no one, with nothing to give you, but oh . . . I love you . . .*"

If that doesn't work, then he turns to a brand of hypnosis and gives me that dark and distant stare right in the eyes, the one he sometimes uses on other animals, like cats, snakes and birds. Now here he be actin' like Barry White: *"Look into my eyes and come to me—I doan wan no excuses. Jus do it! I can make ya—I make cats stand up on they hind leg and spit like llamas—snakes curl up and shake like leaves on a tree—birds fly into thin air just like that. Now, give it up. You want to and you will."* And one way or the other, he winds up getting something.

He plays my best friend when I'm carrying treats. People see him and say, "Oh, isn't he wonderful—he just looks right at you—he really loves you." I say, "Yeah, he's a good guy," lying through my teeth. I can make him dance, walk on his rear legs, play dead, do all sorts of things, like I'm in control of him, which I'm not, unless I've got cookies (the mere mention of which can make him crank his neck around like a chiropractor had hold of him). If I don't have cookies, bring in Idi Amin, Saddam Hussein, Hitler, bin Laden, Jeff Dahmer, or the next guy off the bus, and I become a part of his bone-buried history. I turn into a distant, vague and almost unpleasant memory. Pack Poochy on a plane to France and I'd never cross his mind again, and he'd only take to conning all the French, starting right in at the airport. In a short while, he'd be beginning his days with croissants and ending them with petit fours. Fussed over and celebrated in Parisian cafes, he'd be carried around, supported on the bosoms of rich, sexy, poofed-up French ladies—the guy's a diplomat with skills not seen since the death of U Thant.

Still, my dog's managed to make such an impression on me that I've taken to seeing him in just about everything—the way the Hindus are supposed to with their gurus. In the Hindu Bhakti tradition, the guru is thought to be the "mask of God," and you strive to see the guru in all things; once you do, the mask falls away and God is revealed to be everywhere. There are times, irrational as it sounds, when I believe I see God itself in Poochy's needful eyes. And so, similarly, his likeness has become ubiquitous to me.

Originally, I saw traces of him in every dog, and then other animals followed. My wife and I would see a spider monkey or an otter on TV and we'd inevitably say, "Looks like Poochy." It went beyond small animals with normal faces when we watched the actress Keisha Castle-Hughes kiss a barnacle-studded leviathan in the film *Whale Rider*. When we saw the whale, we simultaneously shouted, "Looks like Poochy!" right in the movie theater, and in that moment I began seeing him in all living creatures. It reached still another level when my wife and I were reading a book, the cover of which was an ancient painting of the face of Jesus, and we said . . . well, you know what we said. He's become iconic, my dog, emblematic of all things loving, free, cute, open, vulnerable and pathetic. We eventually moved on to other objects—anything of beauty: trees, stones, natural formations—"Looks like Poochy, looks like Poochy"—all things looked like Poochy.

Then the mask of Poochy fell away and something else was revealed.

Love itself.

And this raises the question: What is love anyway? Dependency . . . fondness . . . convenience? What? Narcissistic enhancement . . . obligation? Is it duty . . . projection . . . a kind of addiction? Weakness . . . domestication . . . sexual attraction . . . a second job . . . a lie we tell ourselves, or a lie we live until we are parted from life? Is love a precursor to marriage counseling, where we learn to better communicate the idea that "I don't really like you anymore"?

So, what *is* going on here with me and my dog? And also, who am I to say what is and isn't, who does and doesn't love? Maybe dogs and babies connect with us so primitively that it touches us in ways we can't help but to love them back. In our world of adult love, it's not so much food that creates the bond; it's often money, security, comfort, status, or some combination of these, and we just call it love. It's difficult to pin down and even more difficult to keep hold of. Because love, it is well known, turns, with very little help, to disgust or indifference. We are famously deluded by love.

Maybe I'm looking too deeply into it, or trying to figure something that's beyond the mind altogether. But it's confusing when you hear people say, "I love you so much, darling, I want to spend the rest of my life with you and I want us to have a big family." And then the beloved responds, "Oh, sweetheart, I love you too, but I've never really wanted to have children." Now, hold on to your britches because here it comes: "Well then, I'm not going to marry you." Now what kind of love is that? Or, "I can't love you if you're a Republican," or, "unless you're an expressed feminist." Or, "if you don't believe in God." Or, "if you didn't vote for Obama." Where's the love there?

And of course there's always, "I *saw* you texting her with my own two eyes."

"But, *bay*-bee, I just sent her a text, is all."

"Screw you, I hate you! I wish I never met you!"

"*Bay*-bee, what about the last two years, and all the good times? What about our plans?"

"Never talk to me again, you bastard. All men are the same."

So, tell me—where did the love go? I don't get it. Love degrades so quickly into "You stink" / "You double stink" that it makes your head spin like Poochy hearing about cookies. And you know, I think a lot of love does stink. That's why that J. Geils song got so popular. Not so much because it was a great tune, but because it was a great truth. J. Geils himself musta been pretty cynical back then. I've heard it said that behind every cynical person there is a disappointed idealist.

Maybe that's me too. I don't know.

But, the more I think about it, my dog's lookin' pretty damn good. Happy to see me every time I appear. Greets me each morning—watches over me when I sleep (well, not really, but I imagine he does). Gets upset, sure enough, whenever he sees me texting with some other dog, but all it takes is a single head-pat for him to forgive, forget and let the whole matter go. If I yell at him, push him away, neglect him for a day, forget to take him on a walk, or even feed him hours late—he's patient with me— kind and understanding about any and all of it. Twinkles his eyes at me, holds his paw up, smiles (I swear he does) and cocks his head to the side lookin' just like Poochy.

He knows me.

So, he's a food-operated boy. Big deal!

I don't care what I said before. Maybe I'm a dupe. Maybe I've been conned.

But, he *loves* me. Unfaithful companion notwithstanding.

And I love him.

End of story.

The Wild

So, I'd go out to Springfield, Mass. once a week to moonlight as a therapist for an employee assistance program (EAP they call them), serving the needs of employees from Milton Bradley, Smith & Wesson, Electric Boat, Breck Shampoo and other companies. It was the early 80s and I was living in Worcester, working in a hospital downtown, and would go to Springfield weekly with a senior colleague, Dr. Benjamin Bennett, who had been my supervisor a few years before, and who got me the EAP gig. I'd see maybe four or five clients each week and then often go to the famous and ancient Student Prince restaurant in Springfield to eat with Dr. Bennett. I was provided with a nice office, which belonged to someone else during regular work hours, in a private building, where referred employees of the various companies were sent to get treatment for whatever their supervisors deemed they needed assistance with.

The usual, usually: some kind of depression; alcohol—because of a DUI or noticed on the breath at work, or the wife says it's too much already with the drinking; and of course marriage problems of all sorts. One guy came in with his young wife, who was completely gorgeous, and complained that her husband wouldn't stop acting like a dog. A dog, she said. He didn't contest her claim, and actually bit her in the session and she jumped on my lap for help and protection while he barked at me. *Jesus, a dog.* That was very weird, but not as weird as what eventually happened and what this story is supposed to be about. It occurred on a night drive back from Springfield to Worcester. I can't forget it.

There was a young woman who appeared on a late afternoon working the Springfield office front desk. It was her new part-time day job and she had just picked up extra hours working one night a week for the EAP. That girl was hot, and you could tell, untamed, and we flirted immediately upon meeting. So, starting right off on her second week, under the ploy of offering me neck massages (which in themselves were thrilling), we proceeded into greedy, hungry, voluptuous kissing in the few minutes I had between appointments. She'd leave her desk and let the phone ring off the hook like an alarm for us to wake up and stop playing demented children, for Christ sake.

I mean, for *Christ sake*, I was in a suit and tie, and she, young as she was (and I'm thinking 20–21), wore a skirt with pantyhose and heels and a loose, silky top opened to show dewy skin with no pores or moles or blemishes of any kind—the skin of faultless youth—with a business-type jacket over that and lipstick on a mouth that was a dark plum of warmth and want, and makeup on huge eyes. She looked like a gorgeous baby doll on Fifth Avenue in New York, or Rue de Rivoli in Paris, instead of a kid in an office park in Western Mass. trying to make a buck for night courses so she could get a degree in physical education from Springfield College. The two of us looked professional; immaculate in appearance and alleged reputation. But in our minds we were irrational and lewd and filthy little piggies.

Dr. Bennett was more senior than me and had to be more responsible, since he found the job and signed the EAP contract. He just brought me on board to pick up the extra clients that he couldn't see without having to drive in for a second night, which his wife wouldn't let him. He knew I could use the money, and we were friends so he did me a good turn.

Problem was, he'd often pop in from his temporary office down the hall during the 15 minutes between sessions to say hi and hang out. Now that Deirdre (was her name) was there, I figured it was going to be a crapshoot what I could get accomplished with her without getting caught, which we didn't, but my friend grasped what was going on immediately and asked questions in an aroused and appreciative manner. See, he was married and had a few kids already and wasn't getting anything worth living for, or having any fun, except for what I could tell him to keep him engaged and excited. He needed the thrills, or his life would be just a cheerless case of utter domesticity, trying to make do with imagined creature comforts. He would complain bitterly to me on those rides in and out of Springfield, but often ended his rants saying, "I love my family, don't get me wrong; I wouldn't know what to do without them." You know, the way people do right after they realize they're telling you the truth.

The routine was always the same: we'd go out to Springfield in his car, which was an hour-or-so drive, meet with the referrals, leave the office building after the appointments, go to the Student Prince sometimes or straight back to the hospital in Worcester where my car was. There was little time to do anything with Deirdre except for those random in-between-session minutes, which would sadly not be safe from well-meaning and friendly intrusion.

But on the third week, Dr. Bennett couldn't come out, so I drove there alone and Deirdre and I were free to kiss and slop around to our hearts' content and see what could come of it. All the way out there I had half to three-quarters of a hard-on and hoped everyone would cancel their appointments. It was late afternoon in early spring, and overcast, but the gloomy skies and the sinking sun didn't matter because it was all so exciting and I didn't feel too bad about my plan of being utterly irresponsible. I knew, full well, that I would pursue the corrupted enterprise as far as I could, cut appointments a few minutes short, be distracted as a monkey, and parrot a bunch of vacant platitudes to the patients just to keep things moving along. She and I were like animals and I had jungle fever, a case of emotional malaria. And the cure wasn't quinine; Deirdre seemed to be the only antidote.

The two of us wound up on the carpet, because the person whose office it was had Spartan taste and there were a few chairs and end tables with lamps, a small, polished desk, books on shelves, and big windows looking out on the trees and lawns of the Springfield office park, but no couch to fool around on. I had my hands all over her and she, on me, and I was dry-humping her like a baboon while she wiggled under me like a biblical demon, when just then I panicked because I heard people in the outer office. She jumped up and slithered out front, disheveled and without her shoes, to see what the noise was and it ruined everything, even though it was just the cleaning people who forgot and showed up on our floor of the building too early.

Things changed pretty quickly then and the heat got turned way down. We had to wait another week before we'd have a chance to mush around the way we were already just doing. A fucking gyp! We really liked each other. I know it sounds ludicrous, but right away, we did. I had been struck, and though I knew better, somehow I was knocked dizzy by passion and lust.

The next week, I went out with Dr. Bennett as usual, but was griping to myself all the way there because I knew it would be a difficult, clandestine operation to get anything more than a smile or a lick or two from Deirdre. When we arrived, she wasn't even there, and I was crestfallen and became morose. There was nobody at all covering the front desk. After seeing my clients I went to the Student Prince with Dr. Ben, and drank four large steins of German beer and made very little sense, I was told, on the drive back to Worcester. Plus he had to stop three times on the highway to let me pee in the dark, which made him nervous because he had downed two steins himself and didn't want to attract any attention. He had to pee too but held it in. My head was full of Deirdre and my bladder, of urine. Dizzy with frequent urination. Definitely a candidate for at least a few diagnoses which Dr. Bennett was busy working to determine.

I phoned the Springfield office that week from Worcester (and this was the time of no cell phones, no constant, immediate communication, and relationships requiring pretty much guesswork and great patience). I didn't know anything about where she lived or, for that matter, more than her first name. I got nothing but an answering machine, which was not even her voice. I knew she wanted to contact me and would have been looking forward to getting together as much as I was. She did know my last name but I'm not sure she knew the name of the hospital where I worked, and my home number was unlisted. I tried to reach her again, with the same result, then called the main EAP office and asked for Deirdre. They first said, "Who?" and then that she wasn't there, and I said, "Could I leave a message to discuss scheduling with her?" Someone promised to put a note on the front desk with my direct number at the hospital, but I never got a call.

As luck would have it, the next week Dr. Bennett didn't come again and told me that "home demands" (which meant his particularly oppressive wife and wild kids, along with his toothless, declawed but somehow still dangerous Siamese cat whose vocal chords were removed) might keep him away permanently due to his ongoing and intensive training in domesticity, and was I prepared to see all the patients referred, which might mean working until late at night and seeing at least seven people in a row. I said yes because I was feeling despondent and hopeless and didn't much care about anything except for seeing Deirdre. I was a zombie.

When I got to the Springfield office, the note they'd left a few days earlier was still sitting on the desk with her name on it unread, so I knew there was a problem. I wanted to smell the chair she sat in but thought it would be gross because who knows who else sat in that chair, and it would be too difficult to explain if anyone from the EAP or especially a patient came in. So, I didn't smell it, but instead nosed around for the rest of that night and found that she wasn't working there part-time in the days anymore, and they had no information on her that was of any use to me. I felt I'd see her or contact her again somehow, but I never did.

She disappeared. And I believed she wanted to communicate with me but was afraid or couldn't for one reason or another. We'd been out of contact now for two weeks, which wasn't so abnormal back in 1983, but for me it seemed an endless suffering. There would be no company or camaraderie with Dr. Bennett, and now with Deirdre missing, there was no reason to be in Springfield, except for making extra money, which didn't seem worth it. I saw my schedule of referrals that night and went to the Student Prince alone and had their special twice-yearly game dinner of foul, venison and boar, and a couple of fat beers, but nothing seemed to work, not even their famous cheesecake and strawberries. I felt stupid and bereft and guilty and bad and lost, as I often did when I got tangled up with a girl and should have been doing something else with my life, like paying attention to my patients or being faithful to my wife (whom I forgot to mention till now, mostly because I didn't like her very much, but still).

So I took to the lonely, bleak road from Springfield at 10:30 at night, possessed with longing and regret and desire and skull-chatter, when just then I hit the thickest fog I'd ever encountered. It was almost like fabric was laid over the area. Whitish-gray fleece, so deep and heavy I had to stop. Never seen anything like it. Couldn't get anywhere. Plus, I felt like I'd been in a fog all day (felt like I'd been in one since childhood). I was moving under five miles per hour and still having to stop from time to time. It seemed better occasionally to turn the headlights off and just use the parking lights. I saw sets of dimmed car lights pulled over a couple of times, stuck fast in the soup. But, I kept inching along, fluctuating between headlights and fog lights and stopping and going, and found myself on the darkest patch of road. I was hunched forward as if getting closer to the windshield would help, which it wouldn't and didn't. Like leaning forward in a pitch-black room. You just go deeper into the dark and whack things first with your head.

There had been no sign of other cars for some time, and I became suspended there myself, just another jilted machine off the road, fog lights suffocated outside and dashboard lights casting a ghostly pallor in my tiny cockpit, when I had a sense of something at the driver's side window, which I knew was absurd. I slowly moved my head back and to left, certain that nothing more than a combination of my general angst and gloominess was rotating me in that direction . . . and there . . . I saw a huge face looking in at me. It was a couple of inches from mine, separated only by the glass. Though the shock of it froze me, I managed to jump in my seat. My feet came off the pedals and my hands off the wheel and I screamed like a girl in a horror movie. I screamed so loud I frightened myself with my own shrillness. I wanted to stomp the accelerator and take off but I couldn't because I was afraid I'd go right into a ditch on the side of the highway and get eaten by whatever it was. I realized, almost immediately, that it was an animal. First I thought it was a gremlin from *The Twilight Zone* and then I thought it was a llama. I was afraid to look again, but did anyway just to disconfirm my panic, and there it still was, its searching mouth against the glass. I couldn't see anything more than the head because of the fog, but I knew it was big . . . a lot taller than my little Peugeot, with a pointed face much larger than mine. It looked like it wanted in. It actually didn't seem threatening in any way, just there pressing its face into my window, turning slightly from side to side, lit by the dashboard, sort of lost, wandering and wondering in the mist.

Still, idiotically, I continued to scream and gave the car some gas, lurching forward a few yards, fortunate not to hit something or roll off the highway. In so doing I moved past the creature in the window. My heart was pounding with blistering agitation. I nearly pissed in the seat and almost shat my heart out and went on faster than I should have. I was so paranoid at that point that I kept yelling for no reason, feeling like there were roaches crawling up my neck, spinning around looking in the back seat to see if the thing was sitting there staring at me and breathing hot breath on my ear. I practically lost my mind. I swear I could smell its creaturely incense, and feel it rubbing up against me, the way you start shaking your pant legs around and doing a hideous dance when you see a black shiny rat too close at night in the street.

I stopped the car and nonsensically opened the window, poking my head out, yelling into the fog like a psychotic, *"Hey, hey, what the fuck? What are you?"* I should have been terrified to be shouting out there like in scary movies when your head gets ripped off by the monster, and your neck is flopping out the window still squirting, but I knew this was no monster. I knew, even with all the shock and shrieking.

And I saw nothing more of that creature.

After recounting my story to everyone I could, including Dr. Bennett, I was told, and came to believe, it was likely a deer as forsaken and lost in the fog as I was, trying to get across the murky highway and bumping into my stopped car.

I've never forgotten that moment, that face, that feeling. In my driveway the next morning, in the early spring dew, I looked at my car window and found distinct smudges where her mouth had been. The call of the lost wild, always crying out for freedom, had sounded its eternal echo.

And I found myself, once again, adrift in that familiar fog.

Sign

I remember how small I was on this particular day. I was very low to the floor, crouching by the entrance to the kitchen, where my mother, practically still a girl, was standing at the sink with her back to me as the sun shone in, illuminating the chores of her bleak routines.

I was usually too afraid to do anything wrong, but on this day, I felt compelled to risk the consequences of making a mark at the entrance to the kitchen—on the molding. And so I dug my thumbnail into the cream-colored frame, making the sign of a cross, which was the easiest mark to form and represented all I knew of help, or a promise. A way out of the trap of sorrow I suffered for my family and myself. I squatted there and dug in, pushing my nail deeper and deeper into the tiny mark, secretly imprinting my cry. As bad as I believed I was, as much sadness and pain as I witnessed, I was always trying to be good. Maybe Jesus or God would notice this sign; would have been wonderful if one of them did.

"What are you doing down there?" my mother asked, sounding irritated, as she turned to investigate me.

"Nothin'," I answered.

"What do you mean 'nothin'? Don't lie to me, you're doin' *somethin'*," her voice raising to the inflamed pitch I knew well.

I slumped against the wall, my stomach churning, holding my breath . . . and then, frightened, I stopped. Deed done. No one would know. No one would be able to see it, so small and low on the side edge of the molding.

I checked the mark from time to time, to make sure it was there, until we moved a few months later. I was never to return for more than 40 years.

My family had been renting a small two-bedroom apartment on High Street in West Medford, in a duplex owned by Agnes and John DiPiano, who lived above us. We were about to move to our own house in the suburbs. Besides a baby sister, no other kids had come along in one piece yet. My mother lost two after me. She was 30, so was my father. She didn't have a driver's license, and hadn't quite finished the seventh grade, leaving school to work in her parents' bakery in Boston's North End. She was beautiful and thin and considered tall. She was also unhappy, disillusioned, angry and volatile. For nearly eight years I was the only one around to be with her, as my father and his brothers worked 14 hours every day but Sunday in their family business. He was often anxious, frequently exhausted and relentlessly critical. Critical of my mother, and then, over time, of me.

Me, I was lost in thought. But also, just staring into space. Thinking and not thinking. Blank journal with occasional scribbles. Dissociated.

They both loved me, my parents, and disliked one another. And with their love they nearly killed me. Especially my mother, who was triggered to screaming, hitting and other terrifying behavior when she felt provoked. Any disagreement with her demands, or the slightest delay in carrying them out, constituted, in her mind, sufficient aggravation. I was routinely punished by her, and frequently frightened. I lived half the time in a fog, and was repeatedly startled out of it, jerked around like a rag doll. At the time, I was an altar boy, in development to become a model Catholic and for a life spent in delusion and fantasy. In the midst of all this, I felt unbearable compassion for my mother. I felt her pain.

I had no place, power, position or peace, at least not in the apartment. Outdoors, with the rocks and trees and on the streets with my friends, I was okay. Middle of the pack. But home was always menacing, and I was always at the bottom.

I wonder why I made that mark.

Perhaps to save something of myself from that time?

Or to create a future memory?

To say *I was here*, like Kilroy years before my birth . . . or those explorers and astronauts who build cairns or plant flags, as monuments to mark their presence, and existence?

I was here.

And I hope to survive all this and one day return home, return to myself. To recall my immense small-ness, and concoct something bigger, to create something substantial—not just memorable, but unforgettable, indelible . . . a cave drawing, a relic of human frailty and endurance.

And I did return. Made a pilgrimage to the sacred site. To re-anoint. To memorialize the sacrifices made there. To mark the space of crimson-spotted linoleum. To see the sign. Or perhaps I only carved into the soft, painted wood with my thumbnail, and that's it . . . nothing more; then, all those years later, made a story of it. Just to make a story. The world isn't created of atoms and molecules, but of stories. Maybe I wanted to create a world. A new one . . . where I, and we, could be happy and safe.

Making stories from memories . . . I think it has something to do with looking back and fabricating meaning in events that, at the time, just happened.

Maybe writing stories is the same as the tiny sign of the cross in the molding. Perhaps that was my first story, my first memoir, to be known about and read only by me. Now, it seems, I mark the entrance to my childhood with these symbols on paper and share them so others will know I was here, understand me, and help me understand myself, before I'm gone and can't return.

We moved from that apartment when I'd just turned nine, and I revisited long after I'd become a man. It was a different color—now gray instead of white—but other than that, seemed exactly the same.

I ambled across the hedge-lined cement path and up the few steps to the front door, which once seemed so huge, and where I had been so small. I tried the handle and found it open to the tiny entrance, where the two black wood and glass doors still stood. Like a little jail, perpetually dark; the anteroom which served as the holding cell to our home. Our apartment door was straight ahead, and the one to the left led upstairs to the DiPianos', who I assumed were long gone from this life or, at best, in assisted living—the anteroom to the hereafter—waiting to leave.

The metal doorbell was still there, to the right of our door (the door into which I had never inserted a key) . . . metal housing and button—the one I once rang with my tongue because my arms were filled with magazines I collected for a paper drive for Saint Raphael's Church. By doing so I electrocuted myself and was flung backwards and down, where my mother found me moments later, crumpled in the vestibule, frightened, dazed and buried in *Life* and *Time* . . . and *National Geographic.*

This day I used my finger to chime the tolls of my childhood. It was unnerving to perform the simple act, as if I might summon a ghost of my mother or of myself or of any and all those who had visited, lived, suffered and cried behind that door.

Ding-Dong.

And then, while I stood there, still lost in thought after all those years, and still holding my breath, a young woman opened the door to the apartment; nearly as young as my mother was when we lived there, and very pretty. Too pretty to let a man in. Pretty enough to know better.

"Hi, what . . . ummm, what's up?" she asked, not in any way suspicious, but all bright with curiosity. I was immediately taken. I told her I'd lived there more than 40 years before and was interested in visiting. She was momentarily silent, blameless in her disposition of hesitant skepticism. But telling her I wanted to look for something from long ago seemed to pique her interest, while making her even more wary.

Forty years? she must have thought. *What could he be looking for after more than 40 years?* Again, no one could blame her.

From the entryway I showed her my driver's license, and then described the interior, giving details about each room; the basement, the yard, pantry, back porch, and the metal pipe in the kitchen that ran from the basement through our kitchen floor, and through the ceiling to the upstairs apartment. *(The pipe my mother and the DiPianos tapped with knives to signal one another. The tap recipient would open their rear door and shout in the stairwell to answer.)* All of this persuaded her that it was safe to let me in. And, against ordinary reason, she did. She may have sensed him somehow, the one I was looking for.

I was anxious and stimulated.

I walked around the whole place while she followed me, gently and silently, through each room. I knew she was there but I had reentered the dissociated state I lived in as a child. She disappeared and, for a while, became another ghost to me.

I heard the echoes, all of them, even in the basement that still appears in my dreams five decades later. The basement where I hid, and held myself together in the corner, by the furnace. The basement where, under a solitary light bulb, the Lionel train clacked and rolled on large wooden boards with tracks attached, running through a miniature village, puffing smoke pellets through its stack and taking me everywhere and nowhere but round and round. The basement which held boxed-up rockets and decoder rings, comic books and yo-yos taken away as punishments, and a deed to one square inch of land in the Yukon from Quaker Puffed Rice and Puffed Wheat cereals, which were "shot from guns," we were told. That land deed was an ornate, legal-looking piece of paper with a gold embossed seal, containing the very measurements and coordinates of my property, which I treasured but lost eventually through another dramatic and senseless penance. In the basement, I used to imagine taking that Lionel train to the rugged and romantic Yukon to see Sergeant Preston, his horse, Rex, and dog, King, to stake out my land claim and make a life up there with him and the other Canadian Mounties on my square inch.

I was electrified on the visit that day, and sometimes verging on tears.

Remembering the nights where my mother, after those particularly upsetting events of screaming and terror, pushed and dragged me into my room while I heaved and shook and couldn't get control of my crying. She'd place her hand over my mouth to stifle and deaden me, saying, *"Jesus Christ almighty, stop it right now so help me God,"* pressing harder and harder. *"I told you to stop it ... Stop it!"* ... until I managed some stillness and quiet ... by holding my breath ... and disappearing into my mind, which went round and round on the tracks of dullness and fear.

Then sometimes a little later she'd return to sit on the edge of my bed, and seeing I was awake and frozen, would say, *"Honey, it's okay, just think of Jesus and the Blessed Mother. Think of Jesus wrapping you in his red robe and the Blessed Mother wrapping you in her blue one. Just remember them, and don't think about Mommy, okay honey? Don't think about Mommy anymore,"* while she stroked my hair and held me close. But I could not stop, never stop, thinking about her, dreaming about her. I loved and feared her madly, and she still haunted me while I lay sleeping.

The new woman at the old apartment was not troubled, it seemed, by my silent but perhaps palpable emotions, even when, after my tour, I crouched down in the dining room to the left of the kitchen entrance. She watched by the sink, a few feet away, about where my mother had been that day, and young, like my mother was, and as beautiful. I searched the molding with my eyes, and then felt around it, like a blind man, hunting for the slightest trace of an indentation, for even a braille solution to my blind mission. I searched, and then scraped at the paint to try to find the mark under layers . . . scanned every place it could possibly be . . .

But there was no sign.

I sat on the floor, my back against the wall, knees pulled up to my chest, arms around my shins.

"Did you find what you were looking for?" she asked,

quietly.

"No."

"What was it?"

"A mark I made in the molding. An old message."

"What kind of a message?"

"I don't know, a little signal to my future self, maybe. A message left for an imagined me."

"Oh," she said slowly and with kindness borne of sympathetic understanding. "I'm sorry you weren't able to find it."

"It's okay . . . thanks," I said, lowering my head, amplifying my dejection and disappointment to provoke more compassion.

I wanted to say more, to intrigue and allure her with my adventure, my quest, my loneliness and pain. I wanted to say that I was searching for a sign, a promise of homecoming, a development expected—to return and try to reclaim and redeem the ground. I wanted to tell her that it would be meaningful, spiritual, and redemptive. I wanted her to recognize that I was clever and deep and sensitive and different. I wanted her to feel me . . . to make a covenant with me . . . to want me.

To know that I could save her from *her* loneliness and sadness, and take control of things. She must have been in a state of need to let me in. There was no evidence of another there. She was alone.

I wanted her to come to me.

To let me have her.

I thought it would help if I told her I was looking for spectral remnants of my party, there from long ago.

My eighth birthday—I remember the preparations, all done by my mother, who was creative when she wanted to be . . . and liked making a good and special time of things. The dining room, just off the entrance to the kitchen, the large table set with fantastic decorations. Balloons hanging from the lights above and clinging to the ceiling and filling the space with color and bounce, all breathless, and whispering about the party. Bowls and narrow vases filled with M&Ms, poppers that explode when you pull them apart and let fly streamers and confetti, little gift toys at each setting, those woven bamboo Chinese finger traps, and Batman, Superman, Archie and Rootie Kazootie comics rolled up and wrapped in red and blue paper and secured with colored elastics like fancy napkins and placed beside each of the eight settings for me and my lucky seven friends. I knew there was a cake in the fridge, which I wasn't allowed to see, and ice cream in the freezer—vanilla, my favorite. That, I knew. I thought there might be a special present, but having all my friends over on a sunny spring afternoon was more than enough. The entire tabletop was covered with large pieces of different colored paper, which served as a tablecloth underlying all the bounty and booty.

The party was an hour away. I was ecstatic.

To this day I have no idea what was said between my parents, but I remember their aggravated voices and then seeing my mother, enraged in an instant, ripping the colored paper from under the flawlessly set table, and seeing the shatter and cascade of everything on it to the floor. I especially remember the rattle and scene of hundreds of M&Ms spinning and dancing over polished wooden floorboards, bouncing into and out of the corners, covering the dining room and migrating quickly to the living room and in places you'd never think to look. They spun and pirouetted, it seemed, for a long time, or maybe I was just frozen, suspended in shock and grief, holding my breath. Everything was gone from the table except for a few toppled vases and slow-moving balloons, suspended there, like I was, and holding the air in, like I was.

"Look—look what you did," my father said to my mother with a tone of disgust, spreading his arms to display the extent of the chaos, some of the M&Ms still dancing.

She looked at me, all red in the face and eyes, and said, in a cold, clipped voice, "We'll have another party." She seemed irritated with me. I had no idea what I was feeling or thinking except that she was angry with me and that this was a very bad time. I was too shocked to cry.

My father slumped into the living room, my mother rigid as a pole—both of them tiptoed around the disorder and sat in two chairs as far from one another as they could. They both seemed to be crying over the mess and the state of their union. My father said, "Come to Daddy," and reached out his hand; my mother followed with "Come here to Mommy," and reached out hers. I had to choose. I wished my arms were long enough to stretch to the two of them at the same time, but I had to make a move. My eyes filled with tears, and my guts torturously woven, I went to my father to take his hand and pull him out of his chair to my mother. As I went to him, I had my head turned toward my mother, who looked even more brokenhearted and defeated, watching me go to him first. I was a wreckage of guilt as I dragged him in her direction and clasped her hand, pulling her up. They stood in front of one another, very close and very quiet, and I stood between them, with an arm each around their thighs, as I cried and as the spring sun illuminated the gloom. I heard no sound, not even breathing, from either of them.

She moved quickly from that spot, phoned the parents of my friends and said that I'd been feeling sick since the morning and the party was cancelled, while my father sat back in his chair, holding and shaking his head. The pain was concrete . . . the disappointment, stunning.

We never did have another party. At least not one like that. I think we had a couple of cousins over one night soon after, when my father wasn't there, with an aunt, and an uncle-in-law who slept on the couch while we ate ice cream and the few-days-old cake.

I got the special present, a ship in a bottle. A very nice one, which sailed on my bureau top for a decade, until I left home a month after my 18th birthday, still holding my breath. Only by that time, it wasn't my mother suppressing my cries, but me suppressing the growing flames inside. By 19, they had become a raging inferno.

And, right there, in the apartment, I wanted to take hold of this young woman. Take her in hand. Grab her.

Then I thought . . . *Oh dear God, what are you thinking? What's wrong with you? Just relax and feel what's here . . . the memories—that's all they are, things in the past. Just feel them, hold **them**, that's all that's required. What are you going to do with her anyway? You're married. You have a home. You're old. It's too late.*

But, there she was, still at the sink, asking, "Would you like something to drink?"

What a wonderful invitation.

And just then I felt not old, but young, and very, very small, and that it wasn't too late, that the timing was perfect. And from my position on the floor, she seemed huge. I could envision her as annoyed with me. Almost with her hand on her hip, tapping her foot . . . about to ask, once again:

"*What are you doing down there?*"

A part of me wanted to stay, to move back in, to try it over, make it right, make it all work out. Have the party. Lie on the bed, say my prayers, go to the cellar, open the boxes, run the trains, shimmy up the pipe, have my own key and carry it in my pocket . . . I felt she'd understand. That she might need me.

Then the magic occurred . . . as if a spell gripped me and revealed . . .

That she was searching for a sign as well.

I was the one *she* had been looking for.

Looking for me. Waiting for me.

The sign of the cross was leading me to find *her* . . . and was an answer to her thus-far unrequited prayers. Now, this appears at her door, *a miracle. Sent from the past. Meant to be.*

And here, and I can't explain it, I was taken by a great and curious urge. I began to follow it as if against my will. Slowly, I stood up from my folded position on the floor, turning fully toward her. I began to feel massive, and seemed to inflate myself as I walked gently into the kitchen. I held her gaze with soft eyes and a yielding half-smile; I could see her loneliness and sorrow; I could see who she was, living alone there; could see who she might be, and I started to think . . .

I might take hold of her, touch her long brown hair, her neck, and kiss her deeply, pull her in close, breathe on her cheek, and when we kiss, put my tongue in her mouth and into her throat . . . I might even take hold of her throat while I did that and squeeze her down to the black and white floor . . . Press her against the linoleum, with my entire body on top of her, then cover her mouth in case the DiPianos or their successors might hear strange noises. I could easily penetrate her, embrace her, overwhelm her—loving her and choking her down and out. My heart sped up at the thought. It was not so much the act itself, but more that it was all there, before me—there, within reach . . . mere inches away. *I could take control, take on her life or just take her life altogether.* Like a finger on the trigger of a cocked and loaded gun . . . one trivial bit of pressure, an insignificant squeeze, and the world changes into a new world . . . On the top of a building, one small lean, or shift in weight, one sturdy breeze, and the world ends. It was all I could do to keep from opening my mouth to pant. My nostrils had to do the work by flaring to accommodate the rush of oxygen required to feed my pounding and darkening heart.

I think, for the first moments, she saw my approach toward her as amorous. It could have looked that way. I believe I made it appear that way. *(I wonder how many times that's happened? Where the victim, the prey, is surprised by the final action, having supposed, anticipated and hoped for the opposite. Expecting the hand of love but getting, in the flash of an instant, the lunge and thrust of violence.)* I stood in front of her, her hand on the edge of the sink, a look in her young eyes I couldn't fully interpret, some-where between fear and desire, and I told her that *the sign which I pressed into the door molding, a thousand years ago but yesterday, was all I could think to do at the time . . . it was all I knew to do that might save me . . . the sinner . . . the bad boy; to save us, the sad and broken family. And I have been bad, I know it; I've been terribly bad. Guilty of crimes punishable by death. And we all remained sad and broken for decades. And if the sign was not to save me or anyone else, then at least to insure some kind of future. That I'd at least live. And I wanted to live.*

As I told her, she seemed rapt, and I made a sign of the cross, which I traced in the air just in front of her face with my open palm, holding her gaze. It seemed a bit mad even to me . . . hypnotizing her, taking her attention and her mind away . . . and I was just at the edge of something beyond myself. At the edge of a chasm, of time and space, which warped into the doorway of a black emotional crater. And I was walking through that doorway and saw that there *were* ghosts. The place *was* haunted. *I* was haunted. As if these rooms held the love and the lunacy, the memories, the violence and the sad-ness within their walls, ceilings and floors, and the space between them, in their molecules and atoms, which spun and danced all around me . . . in the pipes, which still echoed messages. In the basement that still held boxes in dark corners, and in the asbestos that covered the always-raging furnace, tufting out and beckoning from its cloister to gather, and play with.

I could feel her discomfort, smell her fear, and sense her hope as she remained in place. I had her. Now, again thinking, as with the mark in the molding, *This will always be here in these walls and floors and I'll remember it years from now. Nobody will know. This means something; it means something good can happen now.*

I placed my hand on the edge of the sink; she did not remove hers. I declined her offer of a drink, and once again moved my hand in front of her face, but this time closer, making the sign, blessing her, keeping her in suspense, and under control.

It was all there . . . speaking from every corner, molding, bed and floor. Echoes of the once lived.

Then, I headed, deliberately, toward the vestibule.

I was not followed.

Mochajava

I dumped my cat nine years ago ... my wife's cat actually ... well, she dumped him too—she says she's guilty and ashamed about it; me, I don't know. They were deeply attached. He was hands down the best cat.

He first came to us with an eye infection as a kitten. My wife had serious eye problems growing up, which she still manages, and has always retained a special understanding and sensitivity for those kinds of troubles. To help him recover, she gave him twice daily eye drops and held hot compresses on his baby face. She slept in the guest bedroom with him under the covers for the first couple of weeks, and it was there, I believe, they became as one. Unified in new custody and shared affliction.

In those early days he was only able to open one eye for a while, and then forever after, maintained an inclination to wink, giving him the appearance of a knowing and inside track when he looked at you. Java—so named because of his dark-coffee color—was a Burmese, who could give his paw, come when called, roll over, gives kisses upon request, answer when spoken to and a variety of other feats reserved usually for well-trained dogs. He was a rich, sleek, loving prince of a feline and man did he dig my wife—I used to refer to her as my *kitty mama*. She was, when it came to him, a kind of cat whisperer.

After his eye improved, Java slept with us in a king-size bed for more than a year. When I'd roll over, my full sleeping weight on him, he'd flatten right out, purring like a jackhammer. I eventually developed allergies, which finally required medical treatment, so he couldn't sleep in our bed any longer. But, because of his nature and social interests, Java remained involved in every other aspect of our lives. Our dog, Kena, loved him like her own puppy, and they'd curl up on Kena's bed together on the floor of our bedroom. My wife ended up developing allergies too, and we decided to move the dog bed out to the den, where they'd retire together every night after lights out. We have countless photos of Java spooned against Kena's stomach—both of them, mouths open, bellies exposed—as fast and natural friends.

Java spent mornings on one of the kitchen counter stools, or on my wife's lap while she drank Irish breakfast tea or flagons of cappuccino and read the paper in the sloping sunlight. It was their cheery and contented ritual most days. I know that he liked me too, but I could only spend so much time with him before I'd sneeze and wheeze, have to wash my hands and face and increase the medication dose. Actually, he was attracted to and got along with most everyone. On the rare occasions when he didn't, we suspected that behind the individual's facade of serenity and sociability lurked mad and murderous evils.

Java slept under the covers with friends who stayed overnight. At dinners we'd host, he'd eventually crawl up on the lap of each guest from under the table while they ate, and managed to do it so politely and unobtrusively that even completely cat-ignorant people accepted him as a temporary companion during their meal. We usually didn't know what he was up to until someone said, "Oh, I have a visitor." Never looking for food—just the loving connection he learned from my wife, which she has offered and taught me over the years too. And though I had no eye infection, I was blind when she first got me, and she kept me under the covers with her and made me whole.

My wife . . . my and Java's first love . . . I was his second love, but Kena was most assuredly his best friend. Then Kena died at 15 years old, on her bed, 20 minutes before she was scheduled to go to her vet to be euthanized. We placed her sheet-wrapped body in the car, and the vet handled the disposal of her once-affectionate-and-faithful form. Then we returned with her collar in hand, which was a terrifically heavy weight to carry. It was a gloomy time. Kena had been more my dog than my wife's, and we'd had a long and varied relationship—she was with me through the difficult start of my anxious second marriage, the unexpected death of my father at 61, a subsequent bankruptcy, my wife's father's early death, followed by her three year unemployment and ensuing depression.

Kena was a part of many road races; vacations in dog-friendly hotels and, for six summers, rentals on Martha's Vineyard; a seven-month stint of living at my mother's with me and my wife (along with Java of course and my brother's Siamese cat, Thai—Java's second-closest friend), during a teardown and rebuild of our home; and much more—part of everything that happened over those years of loss and prosperity and anxiety and discovery and aging and life and deaths. She was always present, Kena—silent, stalwart—guarding our sleep and greeting our mornings. Always able to roll with the mood of the house and the individuals in it. Most, most faithful of companions.

At the end, riddled with tumors and beginning to have small strokes, she was still spry enough up until her last day, when even then she slowly tottered down the driveway—low, wagging tail, to say hi and to hang with my and her old friend Tony—who came because I told him she was failing. She even ate breakfast that day—I cooked her some steak as a special treat. And a few hours later as she lay on her bed, which we moved to the kitchen floor to be close—tongue protruded, breathing labored—we called her vet saying she's ready. Dr. Johnson, the only vet she'd known, asked if we could get her there in an hour. We agreed, but within 40 minutes, she was already gone. Neither I nor my wife held her or pet her at the moment she passed. I was in my office next door. I hope she knew I was near and that was okay and enough.

My wife told me that Java appeared at that very moment and spoke to Kena. I imagine that his voice, so familiar, may have gotten through to whatever life energy had not yet left her body. Java asking, "What's up, my friend? What's up? Why doesn't your head move toward me as it has since my first one-eyed look at you? What's up my friend? Want to rest? Want to sleep?" My wife and I cried—the three of us on the floor by Kena's bed: woman, man and cat. As we cried, Java meowed continuously . . . his dirge . . . his woeful funereal chant.

I wished I'd been with her when she passed—and then all my faults and wrongdoing with respect to her began punching me in the chest. To this day, I have

107

guilt about her—about every lost relationship . . . how I could have loved more . . . been better . . . more understanding . . . more attentive . . . more compassionate. How I could have been there, "till the bitter end," as Auntie Emma said about my father's last moments, which I also missed, and how I could have somehow saved them—saved all the gone ones. My father, my grandmother and grandfather; even, ludicrously, Marilyn Monroe, RFK, John Lennon; and more reasonably, my cousin Vic (Auntie Emma's son and by far my favorite cousin). My beautiful, Phi Beta Kappa, Ivy League, Harvard Law School, trilingual cousin. If I'd only been there—stopped by to visit him moments before he blew his brains out on Mother's Day with the first pistol he'd ever held while standing on the diving board of his backyard swimming pool—leaving four very young sons and five letters behind in his doleful wake, along with a legacy of depression, addiction, rumors of lifelong identity issues and a huge question mark hanging in our family. Five letters which carried on the various envelopes the words: *To My Mother, To My Father, My Brother, My Wife, My Best Friend.*

I try to comfort myself with memories of having carried Kena outdoors twice a night for the last months, cradling her 50 pounds in my arms so she could do her business, because she couldn't negotiate the porch steps anymore and wasn't able to hold her water as well as in her younger days. After she'd finished and was back in my arms, belly up, she'd lick my face in the darkness . . . I wanted to cry sometimes when she did, and I'd whisper, "Thank you my girl." And Java comforted her every night in the final weeks, as always—keeping her warm and close and safe—keeping it all familiar. But if I'd carried Kena twice each day for a decade, I still would not have come near repaying the debt of faithfulness I owed her.

After Kena died, Java fell into immense grief (it was astonishing to observe), and hid in the basement for weeks. We'd occasionally hear his woeful wails from down below. He missed her so much that his need to mourn her loss eclipsed his desire to be with us for a while. About a month later, though, he was up again and about his usual rounds—reading the paper with my wife, playing with his favorite feather on a stick, and from time to time going to Kena's corner where her bed still lay, and he'd sniff and speak at it and sometimes take a nap there . . . but he was a little different—reserved—halting sometimes . . . unsure of his new, emptier world . . . dislocated—perhaps a bit tilted. As still more weeks passed, he was nearly himself, and at almost 10 years old, he had lots of life left in him.

A few months later, we got a nine-week-old terrier puppy, and it was that which proved too much for Java. He retreated to the basement once again, frightened and heartsick, and wouldn't come up. We tried everything—animal behaviorists, progressive desensitization, giving him time to adjust—to heal his sense of shock and betrayal. We tried putting him together with the puppy in a closed carrying crate; we tried holding them on our laps across the room to get them used to one another—the puppy was fine and wanted to play, but Java only struggled to leave the scene, and the moment we released our hold on him, he'd fly to the cellar in terror and, I can only image, enraged.

After that, the sole evidence of his ever emerging from the basement was his paw prints on the counter and around the table and sink, where he'd lurk when he was sure that we had taken the evil intruder upstairs with us to sleep. I went to the basement many nights and called his name; he'd slink out of the dark netherworld, talking all the while, and jump into the top basket of his carpet-covered cat perch, where I'd brush and pet him as he squirmed with enjoyment and drooled like an infant. It was wonderful to give him that much, but his hunger and delight in these morsels of attention only highlighted his loneliness. My wife, so occupied with her puppy and guilty about Java's condition, went to the basement to visit him less and less. One day, following six months of self-banishment, we decided he was too unhappy, and that the most humane thing was to find him a place to live happily and with others.

We found the perfect spot. My brother Michael had been forced to give up his beloved cat, Thai, because his fiancée had bad cat allergies. It came down to Thai or her—Thai went, and had been living with a sweet older woman in our town for three or four years. Michael would occasionally visit, but it became too sad for him and, knowing she was happy there, no longer went to see her. The woman accepted Java into her home as well and he now had her and his old friend Thai to live and play with. It was ideal. My wife went once to visit after the initial handoff, and cried afterwards. I never did go. She has refused over all these years to give away any of Java's belongings. Still, there is cat food, still the automatic litter box, the carpet-covered perch, his small bed, a few leashes and collars. Still, the sad and silent museum.

A year ago, Michael got a call from the woman sorrowfully reporting that his dear 19-year-old Thai had died. Now Java had the woman all to himself, and we learned that he slept in bed with her every night, just the way he liked it. She called him Mocha.

We recently heard that the woman died, and I fear Java is at sea. There are people—relatives—living in her home, but he needs a place . . . a place to spend the remainder of his life, as they do not think they can care for him. Though they know him well and like him, they need to sell her house and get on with their own lives. The extent of my worry over this is astonishing—I'm sick about him and feel we have a chance to redeem him and ourselves—an opportunity to assuage fierce guilt—to do what's right and save one of the beloved—so many of whom have been left unsalvaged.

The terrier puppy is 10 years old now. I vote that the untouched basement, once Java's chosen exile, be an option for him. My wife thinks otherwise—thinks he needs "human-on-feline," as she puts it. Love and affection and in-bed-each-night-closeness with a warm, safe body. Maybe so—he was her cat—but I think he'll remember the basement and the perch and the smells and yes, the terrier puppy, but Kena too, and I'll pet him at night again and brush him and make him wiggle and drool once more and maybe my wife will too. And we'll take Claritin and inhaler sprays and so fucking what?

And perhaps in this way he can have a second chance—the terrier has mellowed some, and maybe Java can have his name back and come home again. Maybe home pain is better than strange comfort . . . maybe being alone among the familiar smells and sounds and objects beats being accompanied amidst the unfamiliar. I have always opted for familiar pain. I would rather have something feel like home, even if it hurts, than to find myself among the foreign and other. Or perhaps this is just a theory to overcome what feels like my cavalier abandonment of him . . . maybe 12, or 18 months more with us and he would have adjusted . . . why so quick to say goodbye—to write someone off?

Maybe this time I could really be there at the end—
save him, and in some undersized way, save my father—
save cousin Vic—all the others, and myself, from the
grievous fault of not being there again—missing, once
more, my chance to give comfort and companionship at
the finish.

I know I need my cat, and I think he might need me.

First

I love her but I want her to die first. That sounds bad, I know. I may already be saying too much. Or maybe lots of people feel this way about their loved ones but would never dare mention it; the way they'd never say which kid they like best. Everybody knows who the favored child is, but the parents won't own up. Feels somehow not right to tell that kind of truth. Too real.

I want her to die before I do so I can be there for her . . . a rationalization, you may well say, but still, I want to be there for her so she doesn't have to be here without me. I want to help set her mind to rest with the knowledge that all is, and will be well with me, our dog, the yard, the recycling, her antique plates . . . all of her treasures . . . that they will be as sacred to me as they are to her. That things will be cared for, looked after . . . and that I won't pass out drunk every night . . . for too long. I'll see my doctor, be careful descending the stairs, be gentle with my back, water the plants, and not make a total fool of myself blowing everything on a young beauty who'll drain me and then run off, conflicted, with some buff dope. I want her to feel there's some strength left in my arms when I hold her, to feel the steadiness of my breathing, to finally realize she's about reached the end of her to-do list and that I'll fix what's left undone. I want her to go before me for these and many other reasons. I think it would be for the best.

Maybe just a few months before me. Say six or seven. But then again, they'd be such sad and difficult months, my final ones . . . all the nightly intoxication, the bumping into things, the bruises and swellings—the desperate, staggering attempts to connect with strangers, not wanting to burden friends and family with my sorrows. The daily longing for her voice, the frequent calls to her cell phone to hear the outgoing message, poring over photos. Throwing up. My face blotchy and puffed from all the tequila and tears. Torturous months of how "I should have" and "why I didn't," last words and lost opportunities, mistakes, wanting to take things back, do things differently. Months of bearing the unbearable weight of the real end. Yeah, no . . . those months would be too much . . . too, too much.

Maybe I should cut it way back and go only a few

days after she does. That'd probably be better. But, even those final days spent in heartbreak? What misery! No time to adjust. Just a flurry of agony. No good. No good at all.

Well, maybe then just minutes later. Minutes after she dies, I go. Minutes of heaviness—chest-heaving, numbing depression. Terrible vital shock . . . that alone should kill me right there. What a way to check out, though. Drowning in a flood of pain. She wouldn't want me to suffer like that. Plus I've heard that there's aware-ness which continues after what appears to be death, and I'd never want her to hear or feel my final wailings as I lie with her, to sense my anguish and not be able to respond as she's always done. To have her slip away while anxious about me, but helpless . . . locked-in syndrome at its worst. Unconscionable. Bad for everybody. No, can't risk the dying-only-minutes-later design.

Now, I'd say maybe simultaneous death, but there I'm concerned that I might jinx us into an accident of some kind where we're wiped out early, tragically, unprepared. Senseless death. What a gyp that would be! It's probably best not to send the simultaneous-death energy out there. We've all heard about *The Secret* and such things, energy flows where attention goes . . . you get what you think about, what goes around comes around, etc. So, no simultaneous dying fantasy—bad karma.

Actually, thinking it through a bit, women live 8 to 10 years longer than men on average, and I'm 8 years older than she is—that's a good 16 to 18 years she's likely to have here without me. That's plenty of time for her to recover. Time to resume following the themes of her interesting and well-developed life. Yoga, meditation and jogging, walking the dog with friends, defending the poor, the ill and other marginalized beings, mentoring attorneys who do the same kind of work, hiking with her group of girls, traveling, watching her niece and nephew play basketball and football at their colleges, talking on the phone and filling the house with her laughter and operatic arias for the dog. Plus, she's healthier than I am, eats perfectly, hardly drinks, avoids sweets like poison, eats fruits and vegetables, an occasional egg, doesn't take medications, lives naturally . . . so, she'd probably live 25 years beyond me. We've only been married about 25 years.

She could have another whole life. Plenty of time to find some of the richness and joy we've shared.

Wait! In that time, maybe she'd find a man. Another man? That's an idea. Someone on my side of the bed . . . on my new mattress! Hadn't thought of that. Maybe her hand could warm the sore hip of another—someone sweeter than I am, with more money, a country club member for instance (she always wanted to belong to one of those). Maybe he'd have a sailboat; she loves going off in a boat. I'm talking about a guy who has, at most, a wine spritzer once a week at the club, where they'd go for dinner on Saturday nights with all their new friends. Someone who doesn't think he's so clever. A man with some humility for crying out loud. Not some self-deluded antiquarian who endlessly imagines that beautiful young women still think he's hot. No, a realistic man, a mature man—one she deserves. One who won't swear in polite company. (Me, always saying *fuck.*) One who wouldn't constantly talk about poop with everybody's children (despite it being a favored topic in the 4- to 10-year-old demographic). One who doesn't whip out his dick to pee outdoors at every opportunity. One who would never think to proclaim that religion is stupid at a dinner party, or say "*Namaste* motherfucker" to the new neighbors from Nepal as a joke. A man who would never blow off a fart in yoga class (an obvious sign of looming incontinence), right beside her and her yoga friends, and then start making fart sounds with his mouth to cover his tracks. The new man wouldn't fart to begin with, and if he did, he'd take Beano or Gas-X every day with his vitamins for the rest of his life . . . and not imagine he's some kind of a medical intuitive who could pinpoint the exact reason for the flatulence. No, that man would be mortified, appropriately. He'd be a gentleman.

He'd be a guy who wouldn't say "NO" to every social event in the neighborhood as a first reaction, and then reluctantly squeeze out a "yes" 1 in 10 times out of guilt and love of her and an unwillingness to, once again, disappoint her and her desire to make "happy connections." He'd be a man who would actually *promote* socializing, who would make friends and bring them into her life just the way he does at the country club. He'd take them all out on the sailboat for rides. A man who would finally wear plaid. Brightly colored plaids: shirts, pants and shorts. She loves plaid. She'd buy him a plaid golf hat and he'd wear it all the time. It would be a ball for her. She could have fun for decades.

Maybe her pretty, bright eyes could light his world and he'd be forever grateful and never, ever snap in her direction because he's tired or upset over things not being just so. Maybe she could just relax and never have to worry about his dark moods and manic creative urges, which always come to nothing. Maybe she could be even happier without me. Holy Jesus, what a friggin' gyp!

Then you wonder about him—which one of *them* will die first? I vote for the new guy, no offense! Putting her through the deaths of two husbands does seem unfair. But if he goes first, it might give her some free time, unencumbered time—time to reflect on the good old days, with me. I just can't see him living with her gone. I want him dead. Dead-dead-dead!

In. The. Ground.

Or maybe he should be a lot younger than she is, like 20 or 25 years. She's beautiful and fit; she could pull it off easily. This way she figures from the start that she's going first, and he'll be there all vital and robust when she needs him.

All this stirs the unquiet mind . . . because one of us is going to be in the arms of the other at the time of death. This is true for nearly all of us. There's almost no way out of that. We live together, but we die one at a time. Maybe we all forget that. Or maybe it's the kind of truth nobody wants to tell, such as which kid you like most. Too real.

Okay, now, see how stupid this is? The younger rich guy, Junior, he'd never do this—waste his time while lying next to her in bed, her warm body inches away, writing about who should die first, instead of holding on to her for dear life and going to sleep in her loving embrace before 2 a.m., since she's been asleep since 11:30. And contemplating choking the chicken in the dark to boot.

Y'know what, I'll just write him a letter and hide it in that drawer of unworn plaids I've collected from her over the years. It'll say something like this:

Dear Junior,
    You never met me—something else to be grateful for, besides the outstanding lady I left you. Don't

even think to make her feel insecure because you're so much younger, Mr. Country Club, Mr. 60-Foot Outrigger (Sloop, whatever!). She's the best thing that ever happened to either of us, so you better just sit right there on your balls next to her when she's old or I will find a way to come back and haunt your plaid-covered ass. And be prepared to give her 10 times what I was able to give her on every count or I swear I'll scare you bug-eyed and have you crying for your mother.

Weirdly, as I write this, much as I hate to admit it, I should probably be a little more like you, fucker. In some way, you've inspired me. Maybe even galvanized me to action. Contemplating who goes first and conjuring you up in the process might just make me a better man. It's probably not who stays and who goes . . . but who loves, and who touches, who kisses, who listens, who smiles, who bears the stresses and strains—who reaches out. Not who lasts—not who remains, but who sustains. See? I'm already waking up. So, thanks, Junior, I don't think I'll be needing you anymore, you've been a good teacher and for that I'm grateful. But now, she and I need some time together.

Nuff said. Peace out.
P.S. All the plaid stuff in the drawer is yours.

Yeah, maybe I'll just leave a letter like that.

So, decision made. When the deal goes down, I go first.

Swept

One of the many things my father taught me was how to sweep a floor. I'm good with a broom, and intolerant of those who aren't. I always have one, of some sort or another, at hand. Proper technique requires short, brisk strokes with the broad side, and using the bristles, almost individually, for corners, edges and angles, stepping sideways like a line dancer, a swordsman or a boxer. Your hands on the shaft, capable of feeling and manipulating each tendril of straw. For my father, sweeping was like painting a picture, and the only creative thing I ever saw him do. The well-swept floor was his masterpiece.

This skill was a part of my training in my father's business. He and his two brothers owned liquor and specialty food stores in Boston's Italian North End and other cities around Boston. Much of my childhood and teenage years were spent doing 14-hour shifts on Saturdays, school vacations and parts or all of summers, working for him in various roles in stores, warehouses and on trucks. All this, against my will, which was not a consideration for anyone that I could tell. Not at school, home, church and definitely not at work. In the end, neither was it a consideration for me. I just did what I had to do, and made, as best I was able, a clean sweep of it.

I was expected to sweep the entire store out each night near closing time. It was a very large space with both an upper level and a cellar, which were used principally for storage and inventory. There was filth everywhere. There were rats. I don't know for sure how they affected me, but I know I was not fond of seeing them on the occasions I did. I learned that one bang on the floor with the broomstick caused them to go away so quickly they seemed to vanish. I was not fond of a lot of what I saw, but during sweeps, I did find many coins, a dollar bill, I found a tooth once, plenty of weird, long hairs, which I think must have fallen out of wigs and, of course, lots of dirt, especially in winter. The sweeper got to keep the bounty (a dollar or less), sifting it out from the sawdust, which was strewn on the floor to attract detritus to the bristles.

I learned how to grind up rock-hard cheese rinds—moldy, dirty, rodent-nibbled rancid cheeses of many varieties—and, as my father instructed, would then create a sign which read **"100% Pure Parmesan."** A lie. A dirty lie. And I knew it. Lying seemed requisite for a successful business, and I learned to look right into the customers' eyes and say, "Yes, this is the very best. I wrote that sign and ground all the cheese myself. It's pure Reggiano Parmesan." Clean sweep. I learned about selling the dream and then delivering the nightmare. I couldn't make myself comfortable with what I was doing, but I became good at doing it. Good at sweeping the dirt, and sometimes the truth, from the surroundings.

I didn't want any of this business. I wanted to be with my friends; didn't want to get up at 6:30 in the morning or get back home at 11 at night for a tired and wired wolfed-down dinner on Saturday night. Or to go to nine o'clock mass the next morning and then mandatory lunch with the family before I was given a pass to spend the rest of the afternoon with my friend Steve, after which I had to contend with three hours of weekend homework from the brutal, stinking Catholic boys school I attended.

I wanted an ordinary life. A paper route maybe. Or rake a fucking lawn for Christ sake, how bout? Or no job at all; just school, homework and then playing with friends. That's what most of the other kids were doing, seemed to me. Anything, actually, was like paradise, compared to my program. To hell with something normal, I really wasn't even looking for normal. I envied kids with alcoholic, immature parents who were out of control, but fun. Those parents who slicked back or teased their hair, wore beads and Nero jackets. I longed for those parents who may not have had much money, but spent some of it on Dave Brubeck records, or Elvis, Frankie Valli, the Cascades, the Drifters and doo-wop bands. And though my parents were vigilant, it felt like I was consigned to a couple of oblivious vampires who were sucking me dry without even noticing. I wanted out. I did not want what I had, but there seemed nothing I could do. I have since learned that resistance against what is, is futile.

And what I had was a lot of trouble in school, almost no free time and running around like a dismal rat in those stores. And there I learned the Art of the Sweep. The mesmerizing, meditative mantra of brushstrokes—the rhythm—the roll—the melody of the dance with dirt. I learned to bring it all to me, all the dirt in the environment, with precision.

I also learned about knives, how to use them safely, sharpen and store them. I learned to operate slicing and grinding machines and was adept with these by age 13. I learned to estimate and weigh deli foods, grains, olives and matcha. I learned to deconstruct a 200-pound wheel of Swiss cheese with piano wire and to contend with the gallons of foul-smelling liquid that flowed from the tubes, or what we recognize as the holes, in it.

I learned to carve a cured pig's leg with a long, thin, flexible knife for eventual slicing up as prosciutto. I became good at wrapping things in thick white paper and tying those packages with string. And I learned to serve customers from all walks of life; aged, infirmed, foreign, hurried, frustrated, gangsters, tourists, crazy people and priests. I was able to understand some basic Italian and develop a feel and ear for other languages and accents. I also learned how to scurry away from the store for precious stolen minutes to play with the older kids in the North End streets who said things like, *"Hey, Mari-o, you got a big ahhsshole, you know that?"* and then hustle myself back to business undetected. I was hot to speak and swear the way those kids did, to become part of the dirty street. And I did.

Fuck you!

Fuck ya mutha!

See?

I learned how to handle money, make change, work a cash register and feel comfortable with the loaded gun that lay right beneath it. I learned about people who try to swindle you, and to watch for, spot and catch thieves. I knew which were the Gypsy families (that wasn't difficult to tell); I learned to be suspicious and to keep an eye on people who were looking at me.

I was trained as a guard dog.

My father would say, "Watch him."

"Who?"

"That guy."

"Why, Pop?"

"Because, what the hell's he lookin' at me for? He's lookin' at me to see if I'm lookin' at him, so in case I'm not, he can do somethin'. Watch him, but don't let him see you're watchin' him."

When thieves were caught, it usually, but not always, ended with a verbal rejection from the premises, coupled with the warning from my father or uncles: "I will remember you."

I learned to recognize the deranged, the demented, the medicated and the ones who needed to be. One time that I remember, I was invited by my father to feel the handgun beneath the coat of a "connected" acquaintance of his. The huge, thick man winked at me when he opened his suit jacket to display an oversized black pistol. I learned from watching those hard-bitten guys how to keep calm and remain still while looking at a man who's trying to be intimidating. I discovered the difference between bullies and tough guys. Bullies were babies. Tough guys took care of business. I could tell when a guy had been "away" (which meant in prison) by his pallor and his eyes. Gray and deleted. I could tell when a cop came in for a handout and then left with a fifth of Seagram's 7 or Canadian Club around Christmas. My father was able to recognize ABC agents (Alcoholic

Beverage Commission), and when I asked him how he knew, all he said was, "They don't look right." I learned how to figure it out, how to find my way. I learned to assess the situation. I learned how to move through a throng of people slowly, unobtrusively, nodding occasionally, watching, flickering a faint smile, slipping away or lingering and finally, as always, reading and judging. Eventually I could pick out hairdressers, restaurateurs, anorectics, the depressed, drug users and alcoholics. I knew the affluent and the indigent. I could recognize the suspicious, the neurotics, the horny, the frightened and the angry. I could tell who was alive and who was not, who had juice and who didn't.

This became easier and easier for me to do. My father trained me. He trained me to sweep the floor, and read the room.

It was complicated because he was my hero, my mentor, but I also saw that he lied all day and into the night. Like with the "parmesan," or with the cops he couldn't stand, but pretended to be happy every time one of them walked in for a handout. Or the way he'd lie to the ABC, selling liquor at discount prices, which was illegal then. This concerned and confused me. Whenever I'd bring one of these ethical questions to him, he'd look at me like I was some kind of dummy and say, "What are you . . . insane? You want me to go broke?" He had many dimensions though, and there were numerous angles in the geometry of our relationship. He was an expert, a master, at reading the situation. I'm not an expert, but I've improved.

When I was about 10 years old, I noticed two men eyeing me with interest in the store. I smiled at them, and they smiled back. They were tall, smartly dressed, and approached my father to say hello. I could tell he knew them. He introduced me and they fussed over me a little. My father said, "Sonny, why don't you go for a walk with these gentlemen and come back in a little while." I left with them for a walk down Salem Street; they asked questions, fussed a bit more. They seemed to lean over me like trees as they held my hands while I walked between them. They were very nice. They got me a vanilla cone and then, shortly after, brought me back to my father. He spoke to the two men, and after they left, my father asked:

"Well, what did you think of them?"

"They were nice," I replied.

"Did you notice anything about them?"

"What, Daddy?"

"What did you notice about them?"

"I noticed that they were nice and tall and they were very nice to me."

"Okay, that's good, but it doesn't tell me much about them. Lots of people might be nice and might be nice to you. Can you tell me more about these men in particular?

What did you feel?" He asked in a probing way, determining how fertile my mind was for planting his seeds of experience. I took his question seriously and began to grimace as if I were trying, with my face, to come up with an answer.

"Just say what's inside. Just say the first thing that comes to you." He snapped his fingers and spoke quickly as if to give me an idea of the timing of spontaneity.

"I know, Daddy, they were like girls," I said, mystified at my having brought that idea forth.

"Yes," he said calmly, and I think with a sense of pride. "That's right, they were like girls. They were like girls, and that's why those men are known as homosexuals. You might hear people call them faggots or queers, which isn't nice to do, and I don't want you to ever do that. They are like girls because they like boys."

This notion was lost on me, even though I'd heard those words before, because I liked boys, and I thought everybody did.

So I asked, "What do you mean, Daddy?"

He paused, then said, "They like boys to be their girlfriends instead of girls."

"Oh," I said without getting my arms around it at all. "What do they do?"

"That part isn't important right now, and I don't want you to dwell on it. D'you here me? Don't dwell on it. You should just remember what it felt like, and the next time you get that feeling, you can think, *maybe these men are like the ones Daddy introduced to me*, okay?"

"Okay," I said. And another brushstroke did its job.

And with the brushstrokes, he was painting pictures in my mind, and of my mind, often clearing the dirt, but too often for me—the honesty from situations.

This was my lifelong education, my years of internship. Decades of observation, judgment and training under his guidance. Years of reading the situation, of sweeping a room and putting all the fragments in a pile. Of knowing people, and saying little or nothing of what you know. Making a heap of information I could control, sort through or discard. Now, after so much time has passed, I can guess your age, tell the mix of your dog's breeds, your nationality, your religion, what you do for work, I can tell if you're lying, I can practically guess your name, and sometimes what you're thinking. It's been, on occasions, uncanny. I surprised myself often over time, and then began to trust it.

Some people have thought I'm psychic; I don't know anything about that, but I do know that it's necessary and wise to mistrust my feelings too, otherwise you set a trap for yourself. I've learned that almost anyone can sweep a room after you do, no matter how good you are, and still come up with more dirt. I didn't learn that from my father. He was always one for believing that his thinking was the whole truth. It was later when I learned to doubt my notions. To make a more tentative and gentle sweep of the environment. To walk more softly and carry a smaller broom.

It was on that upper floor of the store one Saturday afternoon—where I ground cheese, saw the rats, and where I happened to be hiding, amid the maze of liquor boxes, in one of the many forts I created for myself—that I saw my father push his own father hard enough so that he knocked him to the floor. I loved my grandfather, my Nonno, and this I could not sift through. Could not fit it all in my pile. Couldn't bang a broomstick on the floor to make it disappear. Here the world began to fold, to collapse . . . the world became unsteady and the ground of existence began to fail.

It was around that time that my father started knocking me down as well, on the rides home at the end of the workday; only he did it with his words. Something had come over him. He was unhappy and didn't know anything about how to help himself . . . he was so duty-bound that he simply had to work, had to stay married, had to attend church and had to play the part he was assigned. No options—just keep sweeping until everything dirty is gone from sight. Those rides with him became breath-holding nightmares, emotional gauntlets to run. And it was worse still when we'd arrive back to the refrigerator of his marriage and our home, which appeared to be immaculate, but was teeming with mounds of concealed dirt.

And then I began to learn too much, have too much in my pile; that's when I found one of the great rugs under which I could sweep all of it.

The magic carpet of fantasy.

And a new life began, a secret one. And it's been grinding in my chest and groin ever since.

A 100 percent pure life. The very best. I know, I write it myself.

Feast of the Hungry Ghost

The deepest need is not fulfilled by power, wealth, position, sex or love . . . revealing hidden parts of the self feeds the deepest hunger.

I was obsessed with the two sisters, and my obsession grew tumescently. I'd just turned 12 when I met them in early spring near The Old Pond where they lived. Their influence on me spanned from my first lurchings toward puberty until I was 18. Their names, Olivia and Debbie— so ordinary and pacifistic sounding—remarkably belied their characters. It's no stretch to say I was a kid with issues. I had been rigorously trained in the catechism of restraint and in the importance of "offering up" desire and suffering to God—but try as I might, I wasn't good at doing that.

Liv was tall, prematurely voluptuous, already tanned before summer, and two years older than me; Debbie was taller than Liv, athletically built, and two years older than her sister. They both had magnificent legs. I could

focus this entire reflection on nothing but those towering
and incomparable legs, which were like perfectly sculpted
living stilts they strode around on, tilting over my tiny
world while peering down through enormous gem-green
eyes—not hazel mind you, but an actual alien green,
which should have been a tip-off that they saw things
through oddly tinted lenses. I couldn't imagine for the
life of me where they came from to be so beautiful, and
to add to their beauty, they were fully hatched teenagers,
while my friends and I were equivalent larvae.

Their father was a pipe-smoking bespectacled man
who was as stiff as Ward Cleaver (from *Leave it to Beaver*);
their mother was tall, big boned and astonishingly plain
(this is the kindest description), with wire-rimmed glasses,
fuzzed-out gray hair and broken-down Jesus sandals. She
was quite unlike her husband, in all his starched crispness,
except perhaps that she had as much body hair. Their
father's appearance was common enough in the day, but I
had never seen anyone else's mother looking like theirs.
(The city of Cambridge, Massachusetts is now packed
tight with women of this nature, slapping around in
Birkenstocks with totally archless feet, white ankle socks,
and bodies composed, essentially, of soy products.)

As for me, I was scrawny, nowhere near tall, liberally
uninspiring, spent a lot of time with my dog—a
humongous and ferocious German shepherd named
Keno—and hung around with my best friend, Steve, who

wound up looking like Ringo Starr eventually and who was just shy of 12.

It was Chuck—Liv and Debbie's younger brother—to whom Steve introduced me originally. Chuck was 11 and a tense, fever-faced reptilian boy who appeared slippery as a viper and had no visible chin (which helped to smooth out the serpentine look he was working with). Chuck was into all things medieval, loved to play war games, build catapults, go fishing with his father, hunt with bows and arrows, and throw rocks at everything. He could spend an entire afternoon pretending to be a robotic invader from another planet. Actually, Chuck was annoying . . . not so much for his interests, but because of his unfortunate personal style, which included the awkwardness of a young golden retriever who could break your leg just playing around, coupled with the mentality of an idiot who could go off at any moment and hurl stones at your head. He was the kind of kid who, in bygone days, would have been the inbred heir of some paranoid tyrant known for his rages and for aimlessly slaughtering thousands, including his wives and daughters, as well as any deformed or demented relatives, save for the chinless Prince Chuck.

Chuck had a tree house in the woods near The Pond, which was extravagant, had a nautically intricate rope ladder and two floors in it, with multiple flashlights hanging from the ceilings. Steve told me that Chuck's father and some other men built it for him when he was nine. His father kept him as a best friend to pal around with; a concept so foreign to me and Steve that we thought the guy was weird and perhaps dangerous. We knew our fathers hated us, and that seemed natural and just.

Chuck went berserk if anybody had an idea that was contrary to what he thought would be fun at that particular moment. We tried not to provoke him in order to prevent injury, and also to avoid having to poke around for five minutes, suppressing our restless smirks while Chuck screamed like he was lit on fire, threw himself on the ground flailing—raging against unreasonable existence—and there he lay—fury on earth. If you disagreed with him about pretty much anything, he considered himself provoked. It was like pulling the pin out of a grenade; before you knew it, BOOM, he was shrapnel—and now, everybody's involved. The kid presented a genuine peril. To add to the problem, he accompanied his father to Korea for three months and surprisingly returned with a black belt in karate. You just know those Koreans gave it to him in such a short time because they were afraid to cross him. Wanting to avoid rankling Chuck was the only thing I ever had in common with Korea, as far as I know.

The doctor supposedly told his mother that Chuck came out of her with an angry look on his face.

Apparently, he was a prophetic infant, knowing from the first day that his parents would be homely, his sisters inconceivably beautiful, while he, always flushed and already zit-faced, would be used as an object of amusement for both sides. Chuck was a force to contend with, but those sisters of his were some kind of hormonal *ooh-la-la*, and way more than we imagined ever having for ourselves one day, so it was worth the pain of hanging around with him just to be near those two girls.

Liv and Debbie were definitely another story, and had mastered the art of torturing younger boys in a variety of ways, since they had been refining their techniques on "Chuckie" (as they referred to him since his birth). They didn't seem interested in going out with boys at the high school, preferring instead to lounge around the house painting their nails, reading, and devising foul and nefarious plans against Chuck and his few reluctant and metabolically distracted friends by casually employing their ample wiles to ensnare us. They were entirely indifferent and nonchalant in their capacity to bowl us over whenever they wanted to. None of us had ever been so outclassed by any girls and were fundamentally stunned and staggered by them, while they remained imperially bored.

They were highly intelligent, venomous bookworms who could entice us into contests that were well stacked in their favor. These were often word games like Twenty

Questions (which they referred to as Thermometer, because they knew one another's minds so well they just had to say "Thermometer" after one or two clues and the other sister would have the answer). We were left to assume they were either psychic or had miniature listening devices embedded somewhere, like the ones Maxwell Smart used on the TV show *Get Smart*. So, they always won, and prior to playing, would compel us to agree to humiliating consequences in the event of our enthusiastically expected loss. Chuck and Steve suffered these consequences deeply, while I only pretended to, because secretly, I liked having to endure them. And there lies the crux of it.

They both frequently said that they wanted to be "dominatrices," and sniggered when they did. I had never heard the word before and, from what I could tell, it was a kind of religious sect they hoped to join one day—like the Dominicans.

From early on, Steve determined that the girls were "a couple of lesbos," and sort of dismissed them as candidates for anything. As if. Not me . . . I began visiting them, often with Steve, when I was sure Chuck wouldn't be around, in an effort to avoid the requisite rock throwing at woodland creatures. The four of us played Thermometer, and card and board games that they always contrived to win. And when they did, they'd challenge our manliness, demanding we prove our worth by doing push-ups and sit-ups at their instruction.

Steve was fairly weak, but had the enviable capacity to say "Fuck it" to every challenge we'd encounter and still manage to walk away, head held high. He was a triumphant loser. He'd begin with a fury and then almost immediately give up (like those fat kids who, after trying in vain to vault themselves out of a swimming pool, flop back and float over to the ladder, grinning). Steve's theory being, "I'm not going to kill myself for a couple of lesbos, I don't care how good they look, man. What's the point?" As for me, I'd try with my last neuron to do well in the games despite generally low potential, but in the push-up and sit-up arena, I had some ability and worked hard to prove myself. I think the girls liked me better for that.

But, Steve was great, despite his physical incapacity; he was not only exultant in defeat, but serenely unproductive day-to-day, having perfected listless youth— no summer job, no hobbies, no pets, no chores. He was the product of wealthy, dysfunctional parents whom he didn't much care for, but who expected nothing from him and, as a result, he was roughly free—free at least to practice his semi-unique rock and roll persona. Steve's parents had no apparent authority over him except that they could make him cry from time to time, usually due to his feeling misunderstood with respect to his need for total and uninterrupted liberty. He was the best kind of friend . . . fearing nothing . . . there were no consequences in his experience or philosophy, and for him things were always just fine. We spent scads of time with my dog, stretched out in fields, babbling mostly about girls, cars, music and our eager futures, while Keno scanned the environment for any hint of threat to either of us. Steve was even able to make *me* feel that every-thing was okay, which was a rare and much-needed contribution for a contracted little being such as I was.

Steve was Catholic, like me, but his parents never went to church, swore liberally, drank fluently, listened to Bobby Darren, Frankie Valli and Elvis records continuously, and allowed him to have a subscription to *Playboy* magazine from the time he was 14. (***Playboy!*** Me, I couldn't get *Mad* magazine through the front door, my parents being relentless fun-suckers.) Steve's folks espoused a variety of Catholicism I might have been able to live with, but as it was, I knew nothing about the sexual world except that it was all grievously sinful and that any hint in the direction of the topic was a source of mortifying shame around my house (my father lived angry and embarrassed about nearly everything associated with having a good time).

Steve had, as did most kids, his own healthy, happy girl-thing going on, which I envied in part because, though about my age, he'd been whacking off since before I met him. Up to the time I was 15, I had never technically done it. Steve always thought that girls and sexual acts were nothing but fun. I thought girls were emissaries of the Devil. I believed that sex was the equivalent of murder; one of the worst and most punishable things anyone could do. My adolescence was spent in a psychic electric chair as condemnation for my thoughts. Steve would say things like, "Man, I got stink-finger three times already this summer and you're still afraid to touch your own pecker in the shower." Only Steve knew these things . . . me, I had a haunted house for a brain.

I was convinced that if I ever touched my dick under the blankets and the cover of night, the Devil and his winged monkeys would fly out of my ass and rush me to Hell after leisurely scaring me to death. Lucifer and his minions would hold me captive in my room, frozen in terror, until dawn, when my parents would find I'd gone missing, with only cloven-hoof prints burned into the rug and the sickening reek of simian butt as a sign that something else had been there, and a tiny cream-colored stain on the top sheet above a huge brown one on the mattress.

I was repeatedly at the mercy of my nightmares. The good Catholic clerics and their zombie associates served as the producers of these autistic horror shows (price of admission: the twin vaccines of sin and guilt—*Bing*—you've got a front row seat). I mean sex . . . straight, plain-old normal sex was an odious and damnable act as it was—now this is just tits, ass and fucking that sends you away to the bad place forever—add anything weird and you're facing an endless sinkhole of trouble before you even get to Hell. The kids at the Catholic school I attended must have figured that I was in line with all the pious twaddle that was supposed to rule their lives, but that wasn't it. Early on I had fixated fantasies, and thought I was alone in the world with them.

A scene I dreamed of was being tied up and held captive by a tall, smoldering, dark-haired woman with stunning, angry eyes visible through a black mask—her gaze, more liquefying than death (like some combination of Cat Woman—played by Eartha Kitt; Betty Paige—the 50s fetish model; and that Wicked Queen who kept popping up in Snow White's mirror). She was far more powerful than me, and could make me do whatever she wanted—and what she wanted was to have me prove obedience to her—by compelling me to perform a variety of degrading behaviors, until she had me prostrate with hands and feet bound—and then stand over me laughing victoriously, calling me names.

I didn't make it up on purpose; it's just the way things turned out. There are, as I've learned, many angles in the geometry of sex. It's a lot to admit, but I had never been drawn by a desire for straight-up intercourse. I had never longed for the kind of girl-closeness and breast play Steve and all the rest of my cohorts dreamed of; it was too dangerous, too perilous for my soul—even, perhaps, treacherous to my mother, who knows . . . can't really say why; I just needed the Dark One to control me . . . I had to be at her evil mercy . . . It was the dominion she held over me that spoke to my body . . . I think it might have been the way I transformed the Devil, converted fear into consolation, and eroticized things that were done to me. I've heard that all "perverse" scenarios are attempts at triumphing over childhood injuries, but whatever its genesis . . . being helpless, ridiculed and subjugated by a dark, dominant and evil beauty were key ingredients.

In the fantasy, I begged and wailed to be let go, but was excited beyond reason and had a sensation in my stomach that I called the "sugary feeling," which was both weakening and wonderful. I first experienced that feeling in my lower belly when my mother gave me paregoric if ever I was sick or in pain as a kid, and I always continued on making a fuss, claiming unbearable discomfort in order to get another spoonful out of her. Finding various substances to reproduce that effect was a pursuit I chased for almost too long, and I was lucky not to lose myself entirely on that road. William S. Burroughs, the Beat writer and famous junkie, wrote, "Paregoric babies of the world unite." I should feel fortunate in having become another kind of addict, but I don't really. There may be some raunchy, tragic dignity in being a dope-fiend, I don't know—but I do know there's no dignity when you need what I needed to get off.

My first orgasm, at age 13, was a wet dream of a scene with that masked woman. I woke one morning in shimmering delight, but thinking that I had somehow peed the bed. Rolling over onto my back, I felt a damp place on my stomach, reached down, touched it and sniffed my hand, and then it dawned on me: *This is it— this is what they're talking about.* **Day of days** . . . It was thrilling and mortifying; thrilling because of the tremendous sensation, and mortifying because I remembered the dream, and now I knew for sure that I was a total miscreant, since my own body had begun to cry it out even while I lay sleeping. Finally, I'd "seen the Lord" . . . and brother, when you do, the Devil ain't far behind. The whole matter was as incomprehensible as it was insurmountable—didn't get it, couldn't get over it.

And so I lay there, night after night, beside my contraband transistor radio, surrounded by the Daniel Boone motif wallpaper and the lone powder horn—my single wall-hung decoration, positioned like an erection up there—while I fretted about how I'd keep all this inside me. Life changed, and all things became penis-centered. Nearly a year later, I finally persuaded my parents to let me move out of that room—which was right near theirs and which I shared with my little brother—into the finished basement, and began going to bed right after my homework was done. My parents were not accustomed to my saying that I was tired so early.

"Sonny," my mother asked, "are you all right? You're going to bed two hours early."

"Yeah, I'm fine. I think I'm just going through some growing spurts, I mean . . . ahhhhh, and yeah, y'know, it's taking a lot out of me."

"Oh, growing spurts, huh?" she replied sardonically. "Don't play Mickey the Dunce with me. Growing spurts, my eye."

My father chimed in, "I don't know what you're doin', but you're doin' somethin'."

"How do you know?" (Where I got the courage to continue the conversation eludes me.)

"How do I know?"

"Yeah."

"Because I was born at night, that's how."

"So what?"

"I was born at night, Mistah, but not *last night*."

She tossed a look at my father which said, *Somethin's* ***wrong*** *with him again.* And of course there was—there was something horribly wrong with me. They were swinging at shadows though; probably thought I was

147

down there trying to get alone to phone a girl, or possibly that it was the beginning of a relapse into a type of agitated and depressed state I'd been in the year before, but they could have had no idea that their Sonny-boy was a little Dracula, living out his baroque fantasies in the dark underground, squirting off to scenes they couldn't begin to imagine and would probably retch in disgust if they tried—Dracula, in the basement, hoping that resurrection from death and everlasting life actually existed—somewhere . . . somewhere in a missing world—one I was only beginning to locate.

In the safety of the cellar, face down on the mattress, I'd begin to fantasize about that woman's darkly painted eyes drilling down into me, while I bounced up and down on my penis, gently and slowly at first, and then more vigorously, until I was soaring around like a trampoline artist, eventually shooting off both against the bed and in the air, managing the whole thing without using my hands—never touched it—I figured that had to count for something. The experience for me was as if I had left Earth itself and set off on a journey to find that lost wonderful world. *(An aside for the uninitiated: Airborne orgasm is an experience beyond compare, to say nothing of the surprise and thrill of discovering the uses of a boy-stick—"polishing the knob," as it's sometimes referred to. If you haven't got one it's not easy to understand the enchantment of carrying so much potential enjoyment, effectively, in your pocket.)* So, I'd scream and laugh and tears would zig down my face until I collapsed in groaning, jibbering, wasted ecstasy, just like those brutal sinners the priests told us we'd become if it weren't for Christ's grace and the support of his one and only true church.

I know now that it doesn't really matter which way you find to jiggle the handle; it's the full flush you're going for . . . and by God I liked my flushes . . . just like all the good Catholics do, and the tycoons, the Holy Rollers, the Indians and Chinese, the priests and the grandmas and grandpas, family pets, movie stars and rockers, televangelists, ministers, fundamentalists, the neighbors, yoga instructors, new agers, hippies, jocks and all the others (except for my parents of course). So, I found my own way to beat the drum to a refrain I just couldn't get out of my head. But nothing's easy.

Immediately after the rush, in the pitch-dark cellar, I suffered enormous guilt, not only because I was committing a "sin," but also because I was doing so under the influence of such perverted images. I was generally a circumspect, scrupulous and anxiously disciplined boy, but when it came to this aspect of my life, I had an absurd lack of control. During this period I took to slinking around my parents as if I were draped in my own sticky sheets . . . wearing the stain of sexual transgression like a freak-flag for all to see. But I was undeniably drawn by the iniquitous dark, and so, went on and committed the grave sin time and time again. It was my daily goal and resort to first bounce into pleasure and then try to rebound out of moral suffering and terror. Now, I not only had a scene in my head, but an on-call delivery system in my pants; I *couldn't* let go of the first, and *wouldn't* let go of the second to save my soul, which, I had been persuaded, was exactly what was at stake.

But, nothing can completely satisfy our longings, so we repeat our attempts. Through fantasy, we enter the screening room of an obsessed mind. And in our private theaters, we watch the show through the projector of our damaged narcissism—where the phantasmagoria transforms weak pariahs into prevailing superheroes, the shamed and shunned into the celebrated, and places us, the marginalized extras, right at center stage; we, the stars in the spotlight—saving ourselves—bounding in to achieve our own rescue. And here, we come not merely to tolerate, but to accept and finally embrace our demons—as if we willed them into life out of passion and the need to survive.

As my high school days plodded along, I began to explore and experiment with my fantasies more and more frequently, lying to my friends and everyone else about what I was doing. I found magazines in Boston's "Combat Zone" that featured the images which flooded my consciousness and sleep. In the cellar I became adept at tying my ankles together and one wrist to the bedpost, then doing the bounce routine. I also became clever at getting girls into stirring conversations in which they'd say things such as, "You are a very, very bad boy. You should be spanked," or "Boys are slime," or "Are you going to make me have to punish you?" A casual comment in that vein by any of the girls of my youth had me floating on featherbeds of bliss.

Once, while living in England for a few months, a beautiful American girl I met on the steps outside a club asked, "What country do you like better, this one or the U.S.?" I replied, "This one." She malevolently shot back, "You're dirt under my feet!" I felt myself weaken with delight and, pretending not to hear, asked her to repeat herself so I could feel it again. She walked up closer, widened her smoked eyes into a wicked glare and, with a mocking smile, enunciated slowly, "You are nothing but dirt beneath my feet," and turned on her high heels to leave. I was delirious with knots of demented excitement, and searched for her through the crowd to continue my exhilaration. When I found her she said, "I command you to be gone." It was great; she was a natural. Statements like that always shot me into carnal infernos. I was an expert at getting girls into arguments, which were always playful, and which led to contrived insults and threatened reprisals. They didn't know the effects they had on me, but I was ceaselessly grateful. The secrecy and anonymity in these situations transformed what would have been unbearable shame into an obscure but dynamic joy.

The fantasies had taken up whole chunks of my personality and I was half the time in a kind of waking dream, which was my shield—what with sex and terror, fear and excitement, indignity and compulsion, Heaven and Hell; it was all so confusing I had to find a way to hide from it in order to endure . . . to breathe . . . to live. I was preserved by dissociation.

Almost everything else in life was uninteresting to me. Nothing was nearly as captivating as this special pursuit, along with my role as undercover superhero—disguised as a pale and twitchy kid, foisting a dazzling subterfuge on a coterie of torment-skewed girls. A superhero, whose special power is getting his covert muscle charged by girls without their knowledge—surreptitiously slipping Kryptonite into their hands in order to feel his strength deliciously melt away. I became so fortunate in finding playmates to join me in these murky theaters that I was, to a degree, satisfied, or so it could be termed, because there was always a dear price paid for it. I was satisfied like a lone wolf having gorged on a carcass buzzards left behind, one who is both sated and sick in the belly with his carrion banquet. I was satisfied in that way.

I inhabited conflicting worlds—hating myself but loving the feelings—unbearable excitement, silent pain. And this drive—this fantasy—my secret, more than anything else, defined my center, and eventually became the reason for so much of my anger and compassion—for my insightful capabilities and unaccounted-for dullness, for my humor and sobriety. It was my deepest truth and bottomless shame, but also grew as a source of bizarre pride, because I possessed this extraordinary "gift of fetish," which provided much-needed distraction . . . from home and church and the demands of my body-mind . . . and nothing, but nothing, took me away like this did. There wasn't anything I could envision that was more delectable than these exotic and forbidden fruits, and mine were perfectly rare and wholly forbidden.

These desires were as psychologically important as they were sexual; they represented something so necessary and primitive that I simply could not imagine my life without them. Though still, I ached to be normal, to want and feel capable of what Steve and every other boy said they desired. I wanted to obsess over tits and ass and fucking and I didn't want to be weird. I wanted to feel what I was supposed to feel, but as it turned out, when faced with many of those "normal" prospects, there was often nobody home downstairs.

A perpetual hope was for my penis to wriggle and writhe to alertness, to be marshaled to geological rigidity at the very sight of boobs and butts and then securely poise itself to convey semen all over the place—I envisioned great lashings of sperm capable of shaking the structures of the real, not the imaginal, world with the monstrosity of their ecstatic force, but . . . no such luck. Little to find down there except for the witches who ruled the dungeons of my inner life. And for this, I knew I was doomed to eternal Hell.

GOD: "I'M SORRY SONNY-BOY, THERE ISN'T ANYTHING MORE 1 CAN DO FOR YOU—I'VE DONE IT ALL—1 HAD YOU TRAINED—GAVE YOU THE SACRAMENT OF CONFESSION, WHICH YOU HAVE CHOSEN NOT TO USE TRUTHFULLY—1 GAVE YOU THE EUCHARIST—MY OWN SON, 1 GAVE TO YOU—HIS VICARS AND HIS PRIESTS—FORGIVENESS AFTER FORGIVENESS—EVERY POSSIBLE OPPORTUNITY. YOU KNEW WHAT YOU WERE DOING WAS WRONG—DON'T PLAY MICKEY THE DUNCE WITH ME—AND YOU KEPT AT IT—DECIDED NOT TO MAKE USE OF ALL YOUR ADVANTAGES. YOU COULD HAVE RESTRAINED YOURSELF—YOU COULD HAVE OFFERED IT UP TO ME . . . BUT, NO! GOT TO HAVE YOUR REVOLTING LITTLE SQUIRTS.

So, IT'S OUT OF MY HANDS NOW.

WELL . . . LET'S NOT PRETEND . . . OF COURSE, 1 COULD SAVE YOU . . . I'M GOD, AFTER ALL—BUT WHEN I'VE DONE THAT IN THE PAST IT HASN'T WORKED OUT WELL AND 1 REGRETTED USING MY POWERS OF PARDON AND STAYING THE EXECUTION OF DAMNATION. END OF DISCUSSION. 1 LOVE YOU! NOW, GO TO HELL!"

(Blackness—shrieking—my mother's face twisted with anger and horror—my father disappointed and disgusted—both of them watching from somewhere. I smell the hot, rotten breath of the evil minions in the darkness. I can't see them, but I know they are inches away. I cover my eyes with sweating palms—I shake—can't move—vomit in streams—a continual flow of diarrhea runs down my trembling legs. I'm covered with icy goose bumps, which begin to itch, then sting—raw hives dowsed with alcohol—a cold agonizing burn . . . The first 60 seconds of Hell—just a thought.)

Though sometimes I was able to momentarily console myself even from that gruesome fate by imagining captivity and torment at the hands of sexy she-devils—I, in the flames, feigning terror while hosting a covert, private ball between my legs—which helped me deal with the thought of facing those paralyzing puke-spewing-slimy-man ones and their stinking monkeys.

So, saying the secret was extremely worrisome for me would be an understatement, because, let's face it, this is not only death and damnation we're talking about . . . this is the very Cock itself, and you don't want trouble with the Cock. One of the many reasons: People right away start thinking you're gay, or worse. First thing: "Cock-trouble?"—"*Gay!*"

You would not choose Cock-trouble if you had a choice about it, **which you don't** *(on this point I stand shoulder to shoulder with every homosexual and other "aim-inhibited" being on the planet).* You have zero option about it. The Cock is by far the most embarrassing and complicated thing to get tangled up with. Truly, what is there besides the Cock to a boy? Nothing. It's the seat of all interest, the focus of adolescent life—it's ultimately the reason for art, religion and politics. It's the godhead, the knob of the universe, the lingam of truth and wisdom. It formed kingdoms and then the reasons for ransacking them; it's the terrible beauty, the pride and shame of mankind . . . and mine, damn it, was not cooperating.

Though, I must admit, I owe nature thanks that my penis was tolerable in a couple of respects—I mean, at least it *looked* decent and wasn't small and, Lord knows, felt great to bounce on—which was pretty excellent if you're gonna have to endure Cock-trouble anyway. At least mine hung right and stood up for something with a girl at the other end of it. So, I was fortunate to actually have some pride in the thing . . . it being furious and humble at once—demon-member and super-spike—both withered with anxiety—and a throbbing baton of stealth pride. **The Cock** ... *what can you say?*

I kept my secrets from everyone in the beginning, even Steve, who knew everything else about me. He suspected something was up though, because of my increasingly frequent absences, as well as a growing pall over my moods, and would occasionally ask, "Hey, bloke, what turns you on, what do you like?" in the Cockney accent he regularly practiced as part of his Ringo persona. I'd say, "Babes, nimrod, what else?" "Fair enuff, but where do you disappear to?" he'd continue, but I'd just shrug it off, always avoiding any probing into my sexual world where, alone, I hid. I wanted so much to blurt out my truths and joys, my superpowers and my humiliations ... I wanted to be open—to be known by someone so I could feel authentic, alive and absolved, but I was to spend decades without benefit of that relief or consolation. And on the few occasions over the years that the secret leaked out from my pants, it became obvious that I was not ready to be known.

One such occasion was when I was 19. I was attending a Catholic university in Canada when I got called back home because of the Vietnam War draft. The story started when I was caught one night by a campus rat (conventionally referred to as an R.A., or resident advisor), naked and trashed at 2 a.m. (as were some other feral types, in various stages of undress) with a chair leg in my hand, popping the frosted-glass fronts of faculty office doors. I'd never done anything like that, and I completely blame foreign beer, marijuana and some kind of pills (which were supposed to make everything go even better than it was already going) for the melee. It was a night of true savage amusement.

To try to save myself from expulsion, I confessed some aspects of my secret sexual life to the Dean of Discipline (a Jesuit priest) that same night, still drunk and stoned and now on a crying jag. It didn't ultimately work—I got bounced all the same at the end of the semester—and not in the good way (*but really, "Dean of Discipline," can you imagine? It's an* S&M *movie title*). And not only did my attempt to avoid expulsion fail, but I was pushed by the school to seek help during my remaining time there. Since behavior modification was the treatment of the day, I was prescribed a course of electro-shock aversive therapy. The Clockwork Orange remedy never ended up working either. I don't believe you can eradicate someone's sexual preference—for me it only seemed to intensify things.

Twice each week, in the research laboratory of a major university in the city where I lived, I was encouraged to elicit orgasms in a small screening room while watching stills and videos of scenes which pandered to my fantasies. This part of the lab was run by the two men who treated me. One of them was the lab director, Dr. Blaize, a tiny man who wore a full-length trench coat and a preposterously huge fedora—I mean huge like from a cartoon—perched over a tiny Pomeranian-like face jutting out of a turtleneck sweater. When greeting him, you found yourself with a handful of damp, depleted digits. But he pulled it off somehow, swishing around all mystery and importance. With the amount of cloth used to cover him, he seemed deep and infallible in antediluvian vestments.

During the compulsory merriment, I was observed through a two-way mirror by the behaviorists, who strategically administered electric shocks through the second and third fingers of my left hand just at the point of climax (my right hand of course being occupied with my dick). I was in a tight leather chair, and the lone window in the room was covered, allowing in no light even at midday. My wrist was locked into a cuff on the arm of the chair, my fingertips clamped with electrified metal clips. The two-way mirror which shrouded the doctors constituted the wall to my left—my shoulder nearly touching the glass. I couldn't see them but I knew they were inches away, and elevated a few feet, sitting over me, watching with their milky eyes in the dark, controlling things, staring at my worried and undressed genitals. They could see it rise, wither and revive—especially when the various witches and dominatrices thrashed about on the screen.

I'd masturbate to the scenes streaming in front of me and was instructed to signal just before I was ready to release. With my eyes fixed on the flickering images, when about to explode, I would shout, "Now!"—*a painful current shoots through my fingers and up my arm—I scream and my eyes rip away from the pictures for an instant of shock and grief. A split second of darkness—current turns off and the screen image shifts* . . . and now, eyes open, there are only smiling, beatific blonds, beautifully coiffed Breck Shampoo types to look at while my spunk is escaping. These girls were light, wholesome and happy in their beiges, yellows and pushed-up breasts. I, in the orgasmic afterglow, sat there gawking at some version of Snow White, having just been ripped away from the Wicked Queen. Now I was bound up before them instead, in all their health—with me splashed dull on the plastic cover across my lap—spent, empty and deeply aware that nothing, at all, had changed. I'd gather my stuff, go back home, and return in a few days for my second weekly dose. It went on for many months. The entire scene was mad, and I felt there could be no more comprehensive evidence of how damaged all my goods were.

Eventually I took the charge as an orgasmic enhancement (I expect the way those people do who like to be choked at the point of climax). I believe the doctors considered my case a failed one.

A girlfriend once flew over from the States to visit

me for a couple of weeks during this period. Madrigal was an unparalleled genius at understanding and indulging my fantasies, and loved doing it. She was a true actress; tall, thin and beautiful, with silky hair that fell to her thighs. The doctors asked if they could meet her, so she joined me once at their offices. She was very free with respect to the fantasy when it came to me, but aloof about it with anybody else. This day was no different and she was not talkative; it was an extremely peculiar meeting—they asked a few questions, and for the most part she stared at them with her dark-outlined eyes and gave them nothing:

"So, you're familiar with his fantasies?"

"I guess."

"And you have carried these out with him?"

(Silence.)

"It's fine, we're just trying to establish the level of your involvement."

"Okay."

"So, you act out these parts for him?"

"What?"

"You act these scenes out with him?"

"I don't act them . . . it's just one of the ways we're together."

"Do you enjoy doing this?"

"What's your name again?"

"Dr. Blaize. Why do you ask?"

"Just curious."

"Anything else you're curious about?"

"Your hat."

"What about it?"

"Why do you wear it?"

"I like it."

"So, you actually like it? Wow."

"Yes, I guess so."

"You're not acting anything out with it then?"

"I don't believe so."

"Okay, just checking."

"Very well then, and could you tell us exactly what you do?"

"I'm a university student in the States."

"No, I mean what exactly do you do with him?"

"I think you already know that."

"Yes, but we'd like to hear it from you."

"Why?"

"Because it might add something to our understanding."

"Look, nobody knows this better than he does and nobody can explain it better."

"Well, of course . . . but . . . we thought . . . you might . . ."

"I'm not interested in doing that."

"Doing what?"

"Spelling out the details."

"Oh, why not?"

"Because it's private and personal and not cool to talk about."

And things continued along those lines, with Mad representing herself in an annoyed but teasing and almost playful manner, drawing her hair away from her shoulder with the back of her hand, cascading it like a slap in their faces. She squeezed my hand once during the meeting and whispered, *"Dinks,"* while they were conferring about the lost cause of their interview.

The younger, single therapist, Jeff, seemed captivated by her. Knowing I was having a party that weekend, Jeff said that he would be interested in meeting my acquaintances—which turned out to be a ruse—and sort of ended up inviting himself. There were a number of friends expected, mostly actors and students, getting together to drink beer, smoke pot, listen to music, and some, of course, wanted to meet the "Yankee Chick." I was uneasy about Jeff showing up—he was kind of a stiff and about twice my height and width. His size didn't square with his job—he should have been something else— something bigger—something requiring more heft than throwing switches and taking notes. He was far more suited to be an Olav or a Sven—some famous boulder- and log-tossing Scandie. I was a skinny 19-year-old, on the way to being a hippie-type actor-failure career- pervert—no match for him. No match at all.

The guy actually did show up at the party, looking especially out of place—with his additional 10 years and straight, starched clothes—got drunk early and made moves on Mad. She came to me and said that he was freaking her out. I walked through the house past the others, told him she didn't like him and didn't want him around. He was embarrassed and before leaving, asked that I not say anything to Dr. Blaize. Just three days later he was back busying himself with frying my fantasies into a failed flambé. Business as usual. (In 1968 it seems professional boundaries had not yet been discovered.)

Still, with all their size and mystery, all the clothes, credentials and prestige, and despite their best clinical efforts, the fantasy remained intact. Plus, I kept the pretty girl. *You never got me down, dinks!* And, after that weekend, I felt myself take back some power—I showed up for the appointments—but enjoyed my squirts like I was reading the Marquis de Sade in church. And sometimes I'd throw their timing off by shouting the warning while already well into cumming to the screen-demons. At this point I knew for sure that it was intractable—the secret was to be forever a part of me, to come to terms with in any way I was able, and not something to be taken away, reformed, reframed or published by anyone in a famous-successes journal. The secret circuitry of my inner life could not be shorted by electrodes. Honestly, they meant well, the docs—you know, shocking people into changing—same idea as slapping kids in the face—didn't—doesn't—won't work.

As for Jeff—I kept his secret, but he and his boss did not keep mine.

When I got called back to the States, Dr. Blaize wrote a letter to the draft board on my behalf, which turned out to be explicit—giving intimate details of my imaginings and saying that as a result I might be unfit for military service *(unfit to kill and die in a tropical rain forest from poison darts and jungle rot, which, had I been unfortunate enough to acquire, I would likely have been overtreating with heroin).* I was glad they were doing their part to keep me out of the war, but I had no idea, when I flew home for the draft assessment, that the letter contained all that it did. I carried that file around the huge Quonset hut, where we were housed for the evaluation, wearing only my underpants along with all the other sheep in underpants, waiting to be fleeced. Some of the potential draftees were gung-ho chest-thumping types with Fu Manchu mustaches and tattoos, at least one I remember was puking, a few were shaking and crying and I think one kid peed down his leg—everybody was bare-chested. Right then I hated life. I was quiet and anxious . . . not a huge shift from the usual mood. It was a warm, sunny, lousy day.

I opened the folder while lined up on a metal bench and read the letter. I was stunned and mortified that my secrets were part of a public document. That fucking dink betrayed me! He may as well have been a living descendent of the Iscariot family. And here I made sense of the young secretary's weird and knowing look when she handed the file to me.

I found a pen and compulsively and painstakingly blackened out all the words and sentences I didn't want read so that they could not be deciphered.

At my interview with the military psychiatrist, he asked why the letter had been edited.

"I didn't want anyone to see it," I replied.

"Why not?"

"Because it's personal."

"I understand that; people who come to me discuss personal things."

"Yeah."

"Then why did you do it?"

"Because he didn't need to say all the details—they weren't supposed to be in there. We talked about it."

"It's part of your draft-board file."

"Well, the draft board doesn't need to know the details."

"What did it say?"

"I'm not telling."

"You have to tell . . . you didn't have the right to do what you did. You defaced government property."

"Too late now, I guess."

"No, it isn't . . . all you have to do is tell me exactly what it said."

"No."

"If you don't tell me, I'll have to assume there's no problem that would keep you out of the military and I'll find you suitable for the draft."

"Okay."

"Okay what?"

"Okay, go ahead."

"I'll draft you."

"I'm not telling you, so . . ."

I was thinking that this particular stand wasn't going to do me any good, but I was ready to go down with it. I didn't trust him or anybody around this business. I could have gone and spilled the beans and gotten drafted anyway. If that happened, I would have just wanted to bite myself, probably would have shot at my platoon leader, or maybe even been part of the Mi Lai Massacre. I practically crept out of the draft building that day to avoid the secretary, who, I was sure, was lurking around, wanting to ask me how it all went, slipping in some reference or other to my dossier. I later learned I was given a 4F deferral for psychiatric reasons. Needless to say, my enduring paranoia had not been unreasonable, though this is one of the times the secret might have saved my life.

On another occasion confirming how unready I was

to be exposed, I was 21, living with five guys in a big house back in Canada, and would phone Madrigal late at night at least once a week. It was very expensive, and would have remained so except that by chance I started a casual conversation with the operator who was assisting me in placing one of those calls. We rapidly became phone friends, and on the spot she allowed me to make the call (and all subsequent ones) to the U.S. without any charge, provided that I dialed her directly on the nights she worked. She told me her schedule and I arranged my calling timetable around it. I was grateful for her generosity and for the risk I imagined she took, so we always chatted for a while prior to the calls being put through. Her voice was incredibly stimulating.

I was now able to take my sweet time on the line and Mad would get me off elaborately during our extended conversations—she, as I said, being an expert at concocting grand scenes designed to make me stupid with excitement. I did not know, but I *was* paying a price for those calls. The operator had been listening in on a number of them and, before I learned that, she expressed an interest in meeting. We did, and she quickly confessed her clandestine activities and having been drawn in by the conversations, especially the unusual sexual play. She said she got excited hearing me climax on the phone while being told stories of dominance and seduction by someone who was so good at it. She wondered if she might be able to do it as well. Although I was completely anxious and suspicious, my curiosity won out.

Her name was Valra; she was five years older than me and turned out to be as attractive as her rich and husky voice. She came to my house a number of times and we drank beer, smoked hashish, went out from time to time and dreamed up and played varieties of the fantasy. She was a natural.

One of my housemates, Mark Trainer, suspected something was going on with me, in part because of the mystery and obscurity which cloaked some of my activities with girls, and also because he was hot for a few of them—Valra was one of those. Mark knew the telephone-operator origin of our connection and, because of his interest in Valra and in my private life, crept around like a stoat one weekend night when I thought I was alone in the house. He spied Valra and me getting high and playing some of the games in front of a blazing fire in the den. As always, but especially during these occasions, my antennae were way up—I had long before developed both pointed and broad vigilance as survival tools. That night, I thought I'd heard something during a quiet moment and darted out of the room, telling Valra I'd return right away, and I found him lurking and skulking by a door in a small hallway that adjoined the room we were in. He acted shy but was smirking, and though older and stronger than me, he was nervous, knowing that I could really go off on him over a breach like this.

He started right in saying all the wrong things: "So, that's what you're into? Hey, man, you want me to torture you or tie you up or something? Cause I will if you want," he said with bravado, the falseness of which was betrayed by the quiver in his voice. I pushed him and threw a glancing kick to his stomach and had my hands up in strike position.

"Hey man, take it easy—take it easy . . ." He was laughing edgily, hands in surrender pose, walking backward, and then he lunged at me. I caught him on the temple with minimal effect, we locked—got tangled up and fell on the floor, where I clubbed at him with my forehead, trying to kill him. Nobody wins with head-butts, but I wanted him gone so I smashed toward his eyes, nose and teeth. He squirmed violently and pushed me off with enormous force, and amazingly dashed into the den, where Valra was stretched out on the carpet in front of the furious fire.

"Hi," he said, trying to sound pulled together though he was breathing heavily, the bruises not yet showing. He sheepishly looked behind to see me as I entered the room seconds after he did.

"Hi," said Val. "Who are you?"

"I'm Mark," he said, crouching by her, extending his

hand, which she took. "I thought I heard you guys in here and I'm sorry if I interrupted you . . . I wasn't interrupting anything was I?" he said with a noticeably sardonic tone behind his toothy grin. He was handsome and built. Friggen cretin.

I felt weak and angry and stupid and naked and confused standing there. Valra seemed charmed by his brashness and rugged good looks. I wanted them both out of my sight, but only after they had been stricken with mutism and intractable amnesia. I told Mark that it was time to say goodbye. He resisted and Valra seemed sad, longing for newfound fun or perhaps more normal sexual activity . . . I don't know, but I hustled him out of the room and he reluctantly left to join the other house-mates at a local tavern, where I knew he would likely tell something. Nobody ever said anything to me directly, but I felt that things had changed. Maybe I was paranoid, but, though the fire in the den raged, the entire house darkened for me from then on.

"He was cu-*uute*," she said, playfully.

I said, "Yeah, okay, time to go," thinking that nothing was cute at this moment.

"Oh, don't be jealous . . . you're cute too, you know you are . . . I just thought it might be fun if he hung around with us."

She immediately seemed unattractive and the portent of endless trouble. I calmly walked over, picked up her thick gray woolen socks and tossed them into the blaze, then eyed the few other strewn articles of her clothing with incendiary intention.

"Hey, what the . . . why'd you do that?"

"I . . . I . . . ahhhhh . . . can't say, really."

"No, seriously . . . what the fuck?"

"It's just time to go, Val . . . sorry about the socks—I couldn't help it."

"Couldn't help it . . . you are *so* weird . . . are you crazy?"

"I don't know, maybe . . . it just freaked me out that he was watching us fooling around . . . you know . . . and I gotta live with him and all of them and I—they'd never let it go. I'm embarrassed about this . . . you know how I was when we first—when it first came up and all . . ."

"And so you burned my socks?"

"I'm sorry, I'm just freaked out I guess."

"I know," she said, "but, you shouldn't be . . . it's fine . . . it's okay . . ."

"I'll buy you a new pair."

"No, it's . . . you don't have to . . . I just think it's incredibly weird and funny you did that."

The conversation went on for a bit, but I was dead inside and wanted it over and done. She was nice enough and sincere enough, but I never saw her again, and didn't make any free calls to the States again either. I've heard there's no such thing as a free lunch . . . I learned that the wisdom of that maxim applies perfectly well to the phone company.

As I said, I was nowhere near ready to open the doors to my private screening room—my internalized safe house. The only ones who ever did enter were the girls who understood my attractions and who themselves became enthusiasts or, even better, were disposed in the direction of dominance games—*Nancy O'Connor, Cynthia Krantz, Joni Moore, India Green, Ruth Anne Donovan, Havana Browne, Imogene Yuma, Ashley Young, Valra Munroe*, a number of others and, of course, back at The Pond—you know exactly who I'm talking about.

Those sisters. A few months after I met them I began seeing them without Steve (who at that point was wearing a ring on every finger and combing his hair right in front of his face, which was an improvement—made him look even more like Ringo and therefore an object of fanatical attention to the 12-year-old-girl set). I also learned to calculate my visits to avoid their parents. During these covert trips to the girls' home through the woods—past The Pond—I had the feeling of abandoning the real world, where the normal others lived; a phantom—walking into the numinous and enchanted—into the missing world I had been searching for—the one in which I belonged— the one I knew had to exist—for if not, this life would have actually ***been*** Hell instead of only ***like*** Hell.

I felt almost nothing sensible during those short journeys, drawn forward as if by a spell—as if a hex had been put on me—until I'd arrive at my destination, keyed up and dissociated but appearing deceptively tranquil and composed. I know I must have seemed from the outside like an ordinary kid, but I felt like a hungry ghost—and I wanted what all ghosts want—to be seen and to inhabit a normal body. Just spotting one of the Sisters from a distance, an article of their clothing, or even merely passing their house caused a spellbound vertigo . . . my mouth would parch—my flesh, crystallize—I was aware of a taste emanating from deep in my chest and a pounding pulse in my stomach—I could hear the blood beat in my ears. Only here did I feel alive but simultaneously out of my body. I was unable to form thoughts or coherent sentences—nearly all capacity for humor left me and I was in a psychic stumble—tripping over my urges. I was linked to the actual world almost exclusively through fantasy and often it felt cold at both ends of The Pond. I was a trembling ecstatic mess on these walks toward the missing world.

Happily, the Sisters usually liked it when I turned up, quietly, in their backyard where they sunned, pedicured and read smart-books on lounge chairs. Once in a while they would send me away, dejected (but essentially in defeated agreement with their choice), back toward The Pond, where I'd sit at the water's edge feeling gypped, and hopeless, but fortunately, too anxious to engage in a personal drowning—whiling away time on the grassy banks, imagining demons and orgasm scenarios until eventually I'd plod home slumped and haggard. And home was misery.

I was routinely punished, beaten and frightened. I remember so much of my life in the house as nightmarish, sin-filled, with screaming marital arguments, and excruciating shame and personal intrusion. At about age five I locked onto a short-lived TV character named Foodini. He embodied my most lasting and steady image of the Devil, which followed me in my dreams even through high school. This demon of my sleep was a man-sized puppet in a tight black suit; long pointed nose; deep-set eyes, forged angry and evil; sharp extended nails; a horrible laugh; the strength of 10 men— moved at supersonic speed. His dream presence in my room froze me . . . left me with no voice, legs or strength . . . left me a syrup of terror—raw liquid dread with no solid body capable of running or fighting or even dying in order to escape him. Foodini (and his horrible cohorts, Nightshade and Pinhead) made my nipples curl and twist with fear—made my body alien to me, made my penis freeze and weep . . . he de-sexed it, made me deny it, made me hopeless, and feel helpless. Helplessness was an absolute enforced compliance in the dream sequences . . . and wouldn't you know, the fantasy developed into helplessness eroticized—fright eroticized—eroticized anger . . . perhaps eroticized hate. I found a way to risk arousal so long as all the requirements were met: helpless, subjugated, disempowered, punished, beaten down, weak . . . dead. And, finally, mercifully, a humiliated carcass with a hard-on. Fun.

Upon reflection, it's amazing I didn't fling myself into The Pond with the aim of dashing my head against a rock, because I was always in some kind of a gloomy fit back then. I was a terribly hyper boy, plus I couldn't sleep—that was additional misery. I wanted to; I had a cavernous need for rest, but I was up half the night and in a nightmare for the other half. Deep sleep, when it did come, didn't seem to matter, as still, during the day, I remained restless, retiring and insecure. Go to sleep—dream of Foodini; stay awake—stumble around like a dope-fiend all day.

The Sisters often allowed the diversion of my inhibited self in their strangely insulated lives, and being that they were superior to me in every practical way, I believe I was, for them, the equivalent of a human squeak toy . . . sometimes you want to play with it . . . other times—not so much. So, on those rare and cheerless days of rejection, by The Pond, I'd sit in agony, captivated by a reflection which did not charm me.

The Sisters were Swiss-German, "a far more refined heritage than Italian," they'd frequently announce. And even though I was a blond and blue-eyed teen with attenuated features, with them I felt like an immigrant peasant dragging a hurdy-gurdy around with a chimpanzee on a leash. Felt like I had nothing to offer them, but they did admire my push-up abilities and took advantage by challenging me to perform privately in their rough and musty attic, while one sat on my back and the other, in an old rocker, with her streaming legs stretched out right in front of me. I could only do a few push-ups before collapsing under the weight. It was thrilling to feel pressed against the floor beneath one and helpless at the bare feet of the other, where I would immediately climax, then lie there inert and entranced following the feverish spurt, momentarily powerless, with a look on my face which I'm sure was akin to a leering moron. They would rouse me from my reverie with shrieks of cruel joy at my vanquishment.

I remember covertly wiping post-orgasmic drool spots from the floor, which had trickled from my sex-slack mouth where my face had just lain, and feeling the accumulated attic dust collect on my palm when I did. I'd clasp it in my hand, hidden there to keep them from noticing, and because it was, for me, a relic of holy ground—proof of the lost wonderful world, which I would psychically venerate as I walked homeward, through the woods, back toward Bleak House.

Those scenes were all I knew of sex, and from that

point on, with the Sisters' help, I reached silent, undetected bliss-bursts in my pants at least once a week for years, and quaked with fear that they (along with God) would know what was going on. *(This was the reason for being such a late-blooming masturbator; I didn't need to figure out how to whack off—I was busy.)* The guilt over these prohibited activities nearly killed me . . . but not quite. Nietzsche said that the gift of death is that you stop dying; my gift was to continue to die.

I'm not entirely sure what the psychoanalysts mean by the term "death wish," but I think now that there was, imbedded in the fantasy, a kind of wish for death. (Years later, girls would sometimes ask, "What is it you like, what do you want me to do?" and I'd respond, half jesting, "Kill me!" Sounds like a death wish, no?)

As time passed, the games between us became more sensual, in a tortuous kind of way, and by the time I was 16 we had worked out a number of regular routines. All of my excitement went completely unspoken—and even though a word was never mentioned, along with the rapture, I experienced cutting anxiety and scorching shame in the face of their silence, which was for the best, having been endowed with such a nervous nature. I was a living wart of worry. Had anything been hinted at, I probably would have morphed into a salt pillar, or turned violent. This must be the reaction of a wounded narcissist: shame into rage—provoked when any core part of the self feels threatened. For some it can result from feeling momentarily overlooked, and for others, public excoriation, but no matter the provocation, nothing's worse than infantile, narcissistic fury—seen it—executed it—not pretty.

Now, I had always thought that their brother was deeply weird (*of course, the question arises: Who was I to talk?*).

One time, in the woods, I accidentally referred to him as "Chuckie."

"Shut up, asshole," Chuck fired back.

"Oh, thanks a pantload, Chuck. What's the big deal? Your sisters call you Chuckie."

"Shut up!"

"No!" I said, ready to face what all of Korea hoped to elude, plus I was in no mood to take any of his shit that day.

"Well, *fuck them* and, by the way, my sisters think you're a freak."

"What?" My voice quivered with the fear of a nightmare come true.

"They think you're a freak," he said, sounding like the spawn of that cranky tyrant.

Everything jumped inside me. I quickly reached down and picked up a fist-sized rock and cocked it by my shoulder. Chuck scanned the ground but nothing was nearby, and he scratched the dirt trying to pretend he got something, but I knew he came up empty. I lifted the rock higher and flexed my left knee into the firing position that Chuck knew well.

"What did they say?" I started to feel the blood bubble up. I was moving away from the pillar of salt option and toward the dark side.

"You're a freak," he said a little softer.

"I swear to God, Chuck, I'll throw this right at your face."

Chuck flinched to cover with his arms and said, "Like fuck you will, dip-shit," his voice raised in the hope of scaring me off with a looming kook-attack.

"WHAT DID THEY SAY?" I hollered, unfazed.

"They say that anybody who would walk around with a dog like you have is a freak. They say he's basically a goddamn wolf, and they say the only thing good about shepherds is that they're German."

I could sense him beginning to cave. I lowered my arm to waist level with my hand slung out and cocked to the side, staring directly into his eyes with a look of destructive determination in mine.

"Don't say anything about my dog," I replied fiercely but with huge relief.

"Hey, I like him," Chuck responded in the voice of a six-year-old, then muttered, "And, hey, just don't be sayin' anything about *me* being crazy anymore, man."

"Fine," I replied, let the rock fall and we turned

together, going off deeper into the woods.

I didn't really have much of a relationship with Chuck at that time, nothing compared to what I had with Steve. But I learned that sometimes people can be like decoys— only in reverse . . . they seem fake from a distance, until you get close enough to find that they're real. Chuck had remained, for me, a kind of cartoon until that day, when I realized that he too was anxious about his mental reputation. And so, life continued and friendships grew. So did the fantasies . . . the sins and the thrills grew along with them.

The girls concocted lots of consequences and games, like "Couch Trap," which led to my first conscious orgasm (following the wet dream). In this game, the Sisters lay on either end of the sofa, with me seated in the center between them, while both scissored my belly with their long, strong legs, squeezing until my breath was gone (and I agreed to cry "Auntie," which was their requirement for release and which, thankfully, didn't always work). Also, there was "Prisoner & Guard," "Warrior Queens," "Rug" and "Chair." These last two may have been their favorites, since they were chosen most frequently as consequences for losing at whichever game they initiated.

"Chair" required the victim to sit on the couch while one of them, seated on his lap, engaged the other in conversation as if the ersatz chair did not exist. They would shift, wiggle and bounce on their human seat, smothering and persecuting every nerve. For me, silence was the obligatory response; spewing off, the sure reward.

"Rug" called for the sufferer to lie flat on the floor while they alternately walked barefoot on his back or front saying things such as, "Oh, I love the feeling of this rug under my feet, it's so squishy and warm, let's try the other side."

The fury of the orgasms I reached could not have been less powerful than those Apollo rockets NASA fired off to visit the Moon. I too slipped Earth's cloister—with my clandestine, in-trouser launches, and my stealth space probe—Apollo in ripped blue jeans.

Steve never did submit to the Rug and Chair consequences as far as I know, but he seemed to enjoy Couch Trap on the occasion I saw him endure it, and he was frequently in on the Warrior Queens game.

Warrior Queens was especially alluring because it was staged outside in warm weather, allowing added opportunities to avoid Chuck's parents. The girls wore denim cutoffs and were usually barefoot, their toes and fingers painted, often red but sometimes fluorescent orange or yellow, as was the fashion of the day. In time, they would dress sexy for the parts, especially Liv. In the earliest incarnations, they'd wear "warrior" masks (*Zorro* or *Lone Ranger* types), making them look ominous, powerful and therefore, to me, more exciting. (When we played it indoors, they'd wear stockings sometimes, but always high heels.)

Played outside, they'd wear long flowing scarves that draped around theirs necks and nearly reached the ground. They even had a kind of German Kaiser helmet poised above their masks, with a dramatic emblem and a chrome spike on the top. What with their greater natural height, the heels and the helmet, one of them would tower over me by eight or nine inches, and the other by six or seven. It was likely a ridiculous scene to behold from the outside, but I found their hugeness to be hideously arousing. Liv was the somewhat shorter of the two, and though younger than her rangy sister, sported much bigger breasts, and with all her regalia she was like a walking Alp, being Swiss-German and all. Her presence made her seem like an empress lording over a hapless slave. In relation to her I felt surrendered, out of control, no longer responsible for anything inside or outside of me. It created a condition of abandon for which my overcritical and worried self sorely longed. In me she inspired abject fealty, idyllic liberation and absolute awe. She was a natural born killer.

It's strange that with all their influence over the six years I spent in their company, I never got to know them in any genuine way. I saw none of the usual emotions that one would expect, never got to hear about their pain or worry, never saw them argue with anyone in their family, never saw them with boys or friends or concerned about themselves in any way—they were isolated beings— apparently self-sufficient. Their striking eyes, which brought so much excitement, could also appear cancelled . . . deleted. It might not be far off the mark to imagine, between the blank, evil sisters and Chuck teetering on the lunatic fringe, that Ward Cleaver and his wife, Sasquatchie, must have done some kind of a job on their kids. But what do I know?

The girls never once, in all our play, offered lips, hugs, breasts or tenderness—and I never cared about any of it. But perhaps somewhere I wished for a sign of their affection, and that I was more to them than mere amusement. One time only I remember Liv saying, "You're good to torture," when we were alone acting a scene in the attic . . . ludicrously, I was seized by immense pride. Another time, she came outdoors just to stand on my butt while I lay on the ground with Chuck and Steve and two other boys watching a spider build a mammoth web, saying, "Sorry, I can't help it." Here, my joy was boundless, and in that moment I felt that I represented an irresistible urge and attraction for her. Except for those two events, there was nothing else I remember in the way of personal notice . . . but I was more than okay with it; while I believe Steve and the other boys who fluttered in and out of the girls' circle of influence acutely felt those deprivations. The Sisters, contrary to Chuck, were actually *like* decoys . . . apparently real from a distance, but up close—stiff, impenetrable, and the masks they liked to wear, fit.

When they played Warrior Queens they were hot to conquer, and I was tormented by obsessive greed to be defeated by them. I could barely tolerate the feelings, and yet had to have them, so, being damned anyway, these sisters were like manna from Hell.

They'd speak in Elizabethan-sounding English. "Thou art," and "Thou shalt not," and "How dare thee?" etc. When the fight games first began, both Steve and Chuck were a part of them. The Queens always had superior weapons, rough-hewn staffs that were long and sturdy. We had to choose the equivalent of twigs for defense, they said, because we were boys and because we were always at least three and they, only two.

They'd begin by making some silly proclamation of challenge to us such as, "Dost thou dare challenge the Warrior Queens? We are Amazons and puny boys are no match for us." Upon this announcement Steve and Chuck would mock them saying, "Oh yeah?" or some such huge retort, and wave their twigs. I too would manufacture some bravado. And the girls would bellow, "How dare thee challenge us, thou insolent fools? Thou shalt be down on the ground begging for mercy soon enough. Take this opportunity to run whilst thou can before we crush you."

The sides would then charge toward each other.

I remember the dust particles kicked up in the sunshine near the banks of The Old Pond. I see Steve, in his Ringo outfit, casually darting around with his twig, yet characteristically bigheaded about his completely imagined warrior skills. It was as if he were performing an interpretive-dance rendition of the conflict, only off-stage for some undisclosed, fantasized audience. And there was Chuck, fighting with vigor, which could only be shaped by a lifetime of sibling abuse—himself, his worst enemy, as he thrashed like a headless chicken, plunged face-first into bushes, got grit in his eyes and inevitably either poked himself with his stick or in some other way drew his own blood. It was farcical and yet epic. I might just as well have been viewing a Cecil B. DeMille movie about the Roman Empire and the Punic Wars. I couldn't take my eyes off the girls, and stood there slack-jawed like a dwarf Gustave Flaubert watching his exotic Salammbo and her goddess Tanit come to life.

I was euphoric seeing them in their getups, screaming war cries, making violent thrusts with their staffs and easily driving the boys back. I too challenged them, to preserve my reputation with Steve, Chuck and any other kids who occasionally joined in, but I did it sparingly. I was so compelled and aroused by the girls enacting their dramas of power that I was transported to that lost wonderful world, my stomach in sugary pleasure knots, my mouth—dry as the dust particles way up in the air, my loins feeling just as high.

Of first importance in the battle was to avoid being taken prisoner, and when one of us was, the others would retreat and devise a totally ineffective plan for their comrade's escape. I implored Jesus and all the saints to be captured by them *(praying to Heaven for travel assistance in the other direction)*. More often than not, I *was* captured, as sacrificing myself for the sake of my friends was part of the Superhero Master Plan. On these occasions, the girls would pronounce me their prisoner, which meant I couldn't run away, possessed by a magical boundary. Their words were all-powerful and served as binding aphrodisiacs. One of them would then pin me to the ground with her staff, while the other ran briefly after the remaining stooges, who headed for the house 100 yards away to recover, reconsider and give Chuckie an opportunity to calm down.

Once in their clutches, they would transform the game into a variety of Prisoner & Guard. One scarf was used to tie the prisoner's hands, the other cinched around his neck to serve as a lead. They would then drag the captive to another part of the woods, around The Pond, to escape detection by the stooge patrol.

During this time of capture, the humiliation was abject and anything could happen. On various occasions, I was made to perform a number of acts of surrender and submission. But it was here that the *slow motion fight* was born. It grew into a lasting ritual.

Ten or fifteen minutes before Chuck and Steve would come for me, and in another part of the woods, hidden by enormous trees and thickets, with my hands now untied and the scarf removed from my neck, I would be required to assume a boxer-like stance, miming a frozen defense, and then be subjected to a karate-style assault. The Sisters would drop their weapons and begin to kick the crap out of me in slow motion—the mauling complete with sound effects, verbal taunts and other abuses.

First, one of them would slowly plant the instep of her articulated foot in my groin, causing me to bend forward, in mock agony, while the other said, "Take that you wretch." That would be followed with a kick to my now lowered chin, requiring me to snap my head back, falling to my knees. A slow motion sidekick, mashing into my face, would send me sprawling to the ground on my back. They would then place one foot each on various body parts, starting with my stomach and then chest, or else one of them would stand on me with her full weight, while the other participated with verbal derision: "Surrender or die!"

As I looked up into their excited eyes, I felt blitzing, mind-numbing surges of passion—fortunately, my enthusiasm always went undetected *(plus, I don't think anyone was looking)*. I, of course, would resist their offer and refuse to submit, partly as it was the way of the game, but also because I hungered for additional torment. I'd make a half-hearted attempt to get up, and as I did, a foot or two would land on my throat and abdomen pinning me, fake-gagging, in the brush. There was, at times, considerable laughter and delight from both sides. My delight, though tainted by the stain of mortal deviancy, was nonetheless delirious.

"Admit defeat and beg for thy life or suffer the consequences," was their imperious offer. I always opted for the consequences (as would a brave POW imprisoned in the Japanese rat cellar of a World War II movie, who might have said, "You'll never break me, you red devils"), and with the barely audible squeak of a "no," I would refuse yet again. Of course *my* reasons were not brave, but hungry, dark and gratefully secreted behind my zipper. Saying "no" in the game was, for me, a kind of sexual aid. Fueled by this minor resistance, the girls' excitement and staged anger raised, and one of them would stand on my stomach, her weight supported by her staff, while the other sat on my chest, pinning my arms into the earth with her smooth knees, threatening to smother me to death on the spot if I did not comply. They would look down at me, long hair framing glaringly emerald eyes, and in these moments, they managed to dispel any shreds of reason I may have possessed, and I was lost in a feverish frenzy of grimy pleasure. I squealed, squirmed, groaned and often came in my pants. It was ecstasy and as heady as my dreams—all of what I was told would happen in Satan's grip turned out to be *utter delight*.

And it was not only the physical pressure and activity that caused the sensations I experienced, but their words, too, enlisted my interest, and their words became my flesh—their words spiked my veins like intravenous libido shots, delivering a lethal-lovely concoction of adrenaline, endorphins and forbidden harvest swirling in my belly and brain, igniting my starved and tender loins. They allowed me to freely enter and reenter what had only been a fantasy world since long before puberty.

Rapture. Is. The. Word.

Right around this time, the sound of a rock whistling through the trees and other evidence of the inept, mildly terrified but infinitely hopeful rescue party could be heard, and the Warrior Queens would release me to prepare for the impending attack, shattering my spasmodic trance and allowing for my reluctant getaway. Soon after, the game ended (as nobody wanted to contend with a crazed and blood-smeared Chuckie, who was in the midst of a brain conniption, and unable to let go of the battle, which for him was a matter of life and death), and what seemed an eternity of inexplicable exhilaration had occurred all in less than 15 minutes. My lifetime of dreaming and worry reaching its peak in a quarter of an hour . . . all in all . . . felt worth it.

The fight routine itself evolved over the years, along with a number of other games, to in-house 10-minute versions, which I played out alone with Liv in her bedroom. Ornamented fetishistically with garters, seamed stockings, stilettos and dramatic, blazing makeup, Liv would throw a few well-placed faux-kicks, impelling me deliriously to the floor, at which time she would stand over me in a victory pose and then torment me with her words and heels until I submitted as her subjugated and annihilated martyr. And again, only there could the body relax enough to let go . . . only then was it safe to risk forbidden arousal. This scene was my most luscious hallucination incarnate and I was glee-struck with unrestrained pleasure in those moments with her. Experiencing Liv in that role made the brain reel, the body rock, and the mind illuminate with pure release. I felt that each orgasm was airborne . . . longed for those sacred moments and am grateful to this day.

These events were extraordinarily meaningful to me, yet the absurdity of the scenes did not, even then, fully escape me. I had some distance from them, which I actually did not want—I wanted total immersion. It's difficult to find; nothing satisfies completely. But that spectacle became the centerpiece of my lived-fantasy life. I never tired of playing and replaying it in my private theater, but was, of course, never lastingly content.

My compulsive attention to the detail of words, dress and movements carried all the marks of a need emerging from the depths, which was never satisfied, because if it were, there would be no reason to re-enact it. As with art, music and literature, once the internal need crying for expression is met, there is no longer a reason to paint, compose or write on that particular topic . . . it just wouldn't come up anymore . . . something else would.

And for me, nothing else did.

Okay, there it is . . . that's the secret, and that's been the battle—the fight inside. Neither the memories nor the feelings have left me, though my interests and capacities have grown through the love I've been given. And now, as I reflect over the many intervening years and relationships, I question if I've caused others sadness or discomfort because of my desires—and though a part of me thinks I may have, and that it's still all bad and wrong, another part, perhaps even a larger one now, doesn't think that as much—but actually that it might be okay, and anyway, can't be helped—and if that larger part of me turns out to be deluded then I'd be upset and sorry. But, I don't want to be scared and worried anymore. I'm committed to walking more courageously through this life with a difference in one of my pockets. Having survived a protracted circuit of aversive electro-shock therapy, on at least two occasions actually caught in my secret life—exposed and maligned by that insufferable housemate, and having been in hiding from all the boys and men through the years, as well as most of the girls, having had to live a double life—I feel I've paid sufficient dues for my involuntary divergence from the sexual standard. I am neither embittered, nor aggrieved . . . and at this point I can say that I'm somewhat released—having unlocked a secret and surmounted a fear, which is one of the greatest satisfactions—facing the fight inside—where the hunger for truth overcomes shame.

And as it turns out, it was not a lost or missing world I found after all, but rather new eyes through which to see the old one. People who see the world through new eyes have been known to get crucified. Maybe you do risk some kind of crucifixion if you don't say, do or give people what's expected . . . and it's the punished ones who are responsible for their own resurrections—nobody else can save them. Help is not on the way. Maybe the scars of punishment become the seeds of salvation . . . we'll see.

Of course, this story is not the whole story, but a vital part of my little life back in The Pond days, and its marks are indelible . . . as permanent as those black spots we were reminded shadowed our souls when we committed mortal sins . . . marks that could not be removed without confession, which was, for me, impossible . . .

Until now.

And now, with the secret revealed, the deepest hunger finds nourishment enough.

Thank you for reading *Beloved Demons*. Now that you know my deepest secrets, I think it's only fair that you tell me yours. Joke. But, if you would like to share your experience of the book, please write a review and post it on Amazon, or Goodreads, or blog it, tweet it, Facebook it, and tell your favorite local independent bookstore that I do a mean reading.

And, if you do want to tell me your secrets, that would be absolutely brilliant.

dramartignetti@aol.com
facebook.com/camstories
twitter.com/dramartignetti
3SwallysPress.com/videos (live readings)

About the Author

C. Anthony Martignetti, PhD, is a writer and psychotherapist in Lexington, Massachusetts, where he lives with his wife, Laura, and their Border terrier, Piper.

He is the author of *Lunatic Heroes: Memories, Lies and Reflections*, and a chapter in *Unlocking the Emotional Brain*.

CPSIA information can be obtained at www.ICGtesting.com
Printed in the USA
BVOW03s2230291213

340464BV00002B/84/P